The Macclesf
& Marple

The Great Central and North Staffordshire Joint Railway

BASIL JEUDA

This is the story of a railway, built in the 1860's and 1870's by the Manchester, Sheffield and Lincolnshire Railway and the North Staffordshire Railway in order to challenge the dominance of their rival, the London and North Western Railway. The author relates the nine-year controversy over the site of a new Central station at Macclesfield, the impact of the railway, and of the Middlewood curve, on Lord Vernon's collieries at Poynton, and traces the competition to the railway from both the Macclesfield canal and from bus and private transport. The rise and fall of passenger and freight traffic, and the use of the railway for holidays and other excursions, are dealt with in detail, and the way in which the railway served local industry is well documented. The threatened closure in the 1930's, the run down in the 1960's, leading to the closure in 1970, round off the history, and the plans to use the line as a recreation walkway bring the story up to date.

Designed by Cheshire County Council
Graphic Design Unit

Typeset by Slanwood Limited, Birkenhead

Printed by Eaton Press

All profits from this book are to go to the Macclesfield Silk Heritage project.

Price £4.25
ISBN 0904532 04 6

The tall North Staffordshire home signal at the south end of the up platform, c. 1954, dwarfs the Middlewood High Level signal box – itself of L&NW design. A. H. Bryant.

Acknowledgements

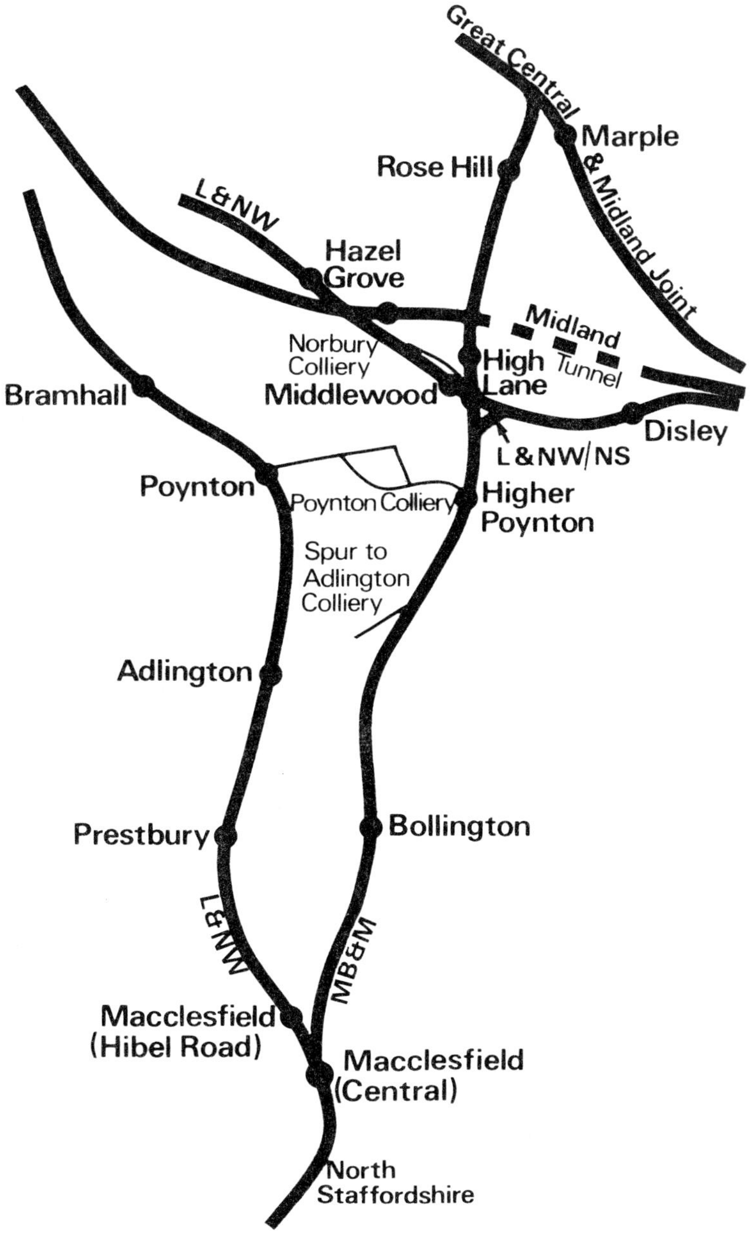

I would like to thank the many people who have helped to make this publication possible – the Cheshire County Council Libraries and Museums Department for agreeing to publish this, their first book on railway history in the County, and to agree generously that any profits be made available to the Macclesfield Silk Heritage project; the numerous railwaymen, former employees of the Macclesfield Committee, the Manchester, Sheffield and Lincolnshire Railway, the North Staffordshire Railway, the Cheshire Lines Committee, the Great Central Railway, the Midland Railway, the London and North Eastern Railway, the London, Midland and Scottish Railway, and former and current employees of British Railways for their personal recollections of life and working on the MB&M; those who have made available for reproduction the photographs in this book and many others besides; British Rail, the Manchester Division, the Signals and Telecommunications Division, and the Property Board; the staff at the Transport Users' Consultative Committee, Manchester; the staff at the Public Record Office, at the National Railway Museum, at the Cheshire Record Office, at Macclesfield Library and generally at Cheshire County Council Libraries and Museums Department, at the Stockport Metropolitan Borough Archive and Library service; the Macclesfield Express and Advertiser; A. P. Carter, G. J. Henshall, D. Rendell, and F. W. Shuttleworth for their photographic help; the Signalling Record Society; the Transport Ticket Society; V. R. .Anderson, A. W. Brackenbury, W. A. Brown, W. R. Burton, R. G. Chapman, G. Dow, N. Fields, G. K. Fox, R. A. Gee, J. Hooley, R. Hughes, Dr. J. R. Hollick, R. Keys, D. A. Kitching, W. O. Russell, J. M. Ryan, W. H. Shercliff, R. A. Simpson, W. J. Skillern, I. R. Smith, J. W. Sutherland, J. R. Thomas, A. St. G. Walsh and M. Welch, for access to their own private research material and photographic collections; K. Maddrell and the draughting staff for the design of the book and for their infinite patience in drawing the maps in the book; R. A. Simpson for his comments on the text and captions and for patiently reading the manuscripts; J. Roberts and J. Myerscough for typing and re-typing the text.

Basil Jeuda,
Macclesfield.
August 1983.

LMS Standard Type 90, 25 cwt., Single Horse Parcel Van at Wolverton when newly painted, April 1925. H. N. Twells collection.

BOOKS BY THE SAME AUTHOR:

The Leek, Caldon and Waterhouses Railway, *published by the North Staffordshire Railway (1978) Limited, Cheddleton Station, near Leek.*

Railways of the Macclesfield District *to be published by Wyvern Publishing, Skipton in the spring of 1984.*

Contents

COVER
Robinson-designed 4-6-2T, GC Class A5, 69828, on a Manchester to Macclesfield local, coming on to the MB&M at Marple Wharf Junction on 25 May 1957. The signal box, to a later Midland Railway design, can be seen at the background. N. Fields.

BACK COVER
The Worthington family were carters at Bollington for many years. This photograph c. 1915, of Mr. Worthington, is taken outside the goods shed at Bollington. The tarpaulin bears the initials GC&NSR. Worthington Family Collection.

With Lower Heys mill, Macclesfield, in the background, the driver and fireman, and shunters pose in front of NS 0-6-0T, D Class, 153. Author's collection.

LNE Sentinel coal-fired steam car "Commerce" in Central station, c. 1937. Note the newly built signal box, to standard LMS design, in the background. The colour of this class of locomotive was green and cream. E. R. Morten.

Former GC 0-6-0 J11, 64382, passes Middlewood High Level box with a Manchester to Macclesfield local on 23 August 1952. The signal box is of L&NW design with McKenzie and Holland instruments, and the signal of NS design. To the right is the former L&NW and NS jointly owned Middlewood Curve and exchange sidings.

The opening day services. Note the incorrect spelling of the MB&M. British Rail.

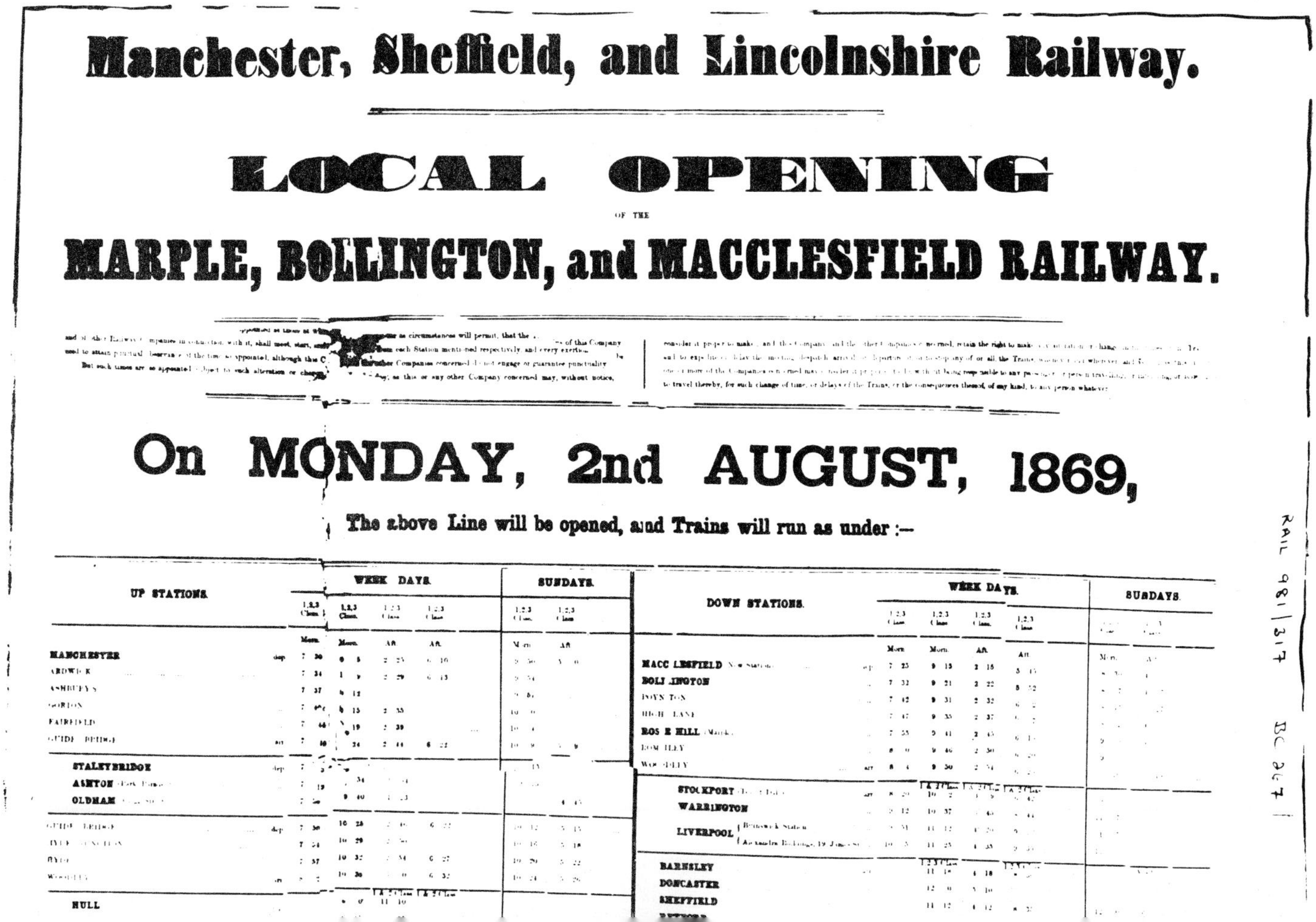
Manchester, Sheffield, and Lincolnshire Railway.

LOCAL OPENING

OF THE

MARPLE, BOLLINGTON, and MACCLESFIELD RAILWAY.

On MONDAY, 2nd AUGUST, 1869,

The above Line will be opened, and Trains will run as under :—

UP STATIONS.		WEEK DAYS. 1,2,3 Class. Morn.	1,2,3 Class. Morn.	1,2,3 Class. Aft.	1,2,3 Class. Aft.	SUNDAYS. 1,2,3 Class. Morn.	1,2,3 Class. Aft.
MANCHESTER	dep	7 30	9 5	2 25	6 10	[illegible]	[illegible]
ARDWICK		7 34	9 9	2 29	6 13	[illegible]	
ASHBURYS		7 37	9 12			[illegible]	
GORTON		7 40	9 15	2 35		10 0	
FAIRFIELD		7 44	9 19	2 39		10 4	
GUIDE BRIDGE	arr	7 46	9 24	2 44	6 22	10 9	[illegible]
STALEYBRIDGE	dep	[illegible]	[illegible]			[illegible]	
ASHTON		7 19	9 34	[illegible]			
OLDHAM		[illegible]	9 40	[illegible]			4 45
GUIDE BRIDGE	dep	7 50	10 25	[illegible]	6 22	10 12	5 15
HYDE JUNCTION		7 54	10 29	[illegible]		10 16	5 18
HYDE		7 57	10 32	[illegible]	6 27	10 20	5 22
WOODLEY	arr	[illegible]	10 36	[illegible]	6 32	10 24	5 26
HULL			[illegible]	11 10			

DOWN STATIONS.		WEEK DAYS. 1,2,3 Class. Morn.	1,2,3 Class. Morn.	1,2,3 Class. Aft.	1,2,3 Class. Aft.	SUNDAYS. Morn.	Aft.
MACCLESFIELD New Station	dep	7 25	9 15	2 15	5 45	[illegible]	[illegible]
BOLLINGTON		7 32	9 21	2 22	5 52	[illegible]	[illegible]
POYNTON		7 42	9 31	2 32	[illegible]	[illegible]	[illegible]
HIGH LANE		7 47	9 35	2 37	[illegible]	[illegible]	[illegible]
ROSE HILL (Marple)		7 55	9 41	2 45	[illegible]	[illegible]	[illegible]
ROMILEY		8 0	9 46	2 50	[illegible]	[illegible]	
WOODLEY	arr	8 4	9 50	2 54	[illegible]		
STOCKPORT	arr	8 20	10 2	[illegible]	[illegible]		
WARRINGTON		[illegible]	10 37	[illegible]	[illegible]		
LIVERPOOL Brunswick Station		[illegible]	11 12	[illegible]	[illegible]		
LIVERPOOL Alexandra Buildings, 19 James St		[illegible]	11 25	4 35	[illegible]		
BARNSLEY			11 18	4 18	[illegible]		
DONCASTER			12 0	[illegible]			
SHEFFIELD			11 12	4 12	[illegible]		

1 Railway Developments up to 1863

Before turning to the history of the Macclesfield, Bollington and Marple Railway (MB&M), it is important to look at the development, prior to 1863, of the railway network in the area, and, in particular, along what was to become the MB&M route from Macclesfield, through Bollington, Poynton, Middlewood, and High Lane, to Marple.

The development of the railway system to Macclesfield started with the incorporation of the Manchester and Birmingham Railway (M&B) on 30 June 1837. The M&B Act provided for a line from Manchester through Stockport, Alderley, Congleton and the Potteries to Tamworth and Rugby, with branches from Alderley to Crewe and from Stockport to Macclesfield. At the time there were also competing schemes from the promoters of the Manchester and Cheshire Junction Railway (who wanted to build a line through Stockport and Wilmslow to Crewe) and of the Manchester South Union (who planned a railway through Macclesfield and the Potteries). The compromise between the various parties led to the route of the main line being between Manchester and Crewe, via Stockport, the route of the branch line being from Stockport to Macclesfield, and the Alderley to Congleton line being abandoned.

Locally, links with the M&B were established in October 1837, when Thomas Ashworth, agent to Lord Vernon, of Poynton Collieries, attended a meeting of the Board to discuss the possibility of a branch railway to serve the collieries; the mutal interest of the railway company and Lord Vernon were obvious, extra traffic for the railways and better markets for coal.

Although the Manchester to Crewe line was completed and opened in 1842, trains were running on part of it in 1840. A trade depression caused delays in building the line from Stockport to Macclesfield. The first part of the branch to Macclesfield, from Cheadle Hulme to Prince Pit (Poynton), was opened to coal traffic on 9 June 1845, and the second part, from Poynton to a temporary terminus in Macclesfield (Beech Road) for passenger and goods traffic on 24 November 1845; intermediate stations at Poynton (Midway), Adlington and Prestbury, were opened at the same time.

In the meantime, interests in the Potteries were successful in securing the passage through Parliament on 26 June 1846 of 3 separate North Staffordshire Railway (NS) Acts which thereby provided the NS with its backbone for future developments. The Pottery Line Act sanctioned the line from Macclesfield through Stoke to Colwich, whilst the Churnet Valley Act sanctioned the line from North Rode to Uttoxeter. The section of line from Congleton to Macclesfield was opened on 18 June 1849, and the following month saw the closure of the temporary station at Beech Road with the opening, on 13 July 1849, of Hibel Road station and of the Churnet Valley line.

Hibel Road station was jointly owned by the London and North Western Railway (L&NW) and the NS. The former came into existence in 1846 from the amalgamation of the Grand Junction Railway, the London and Birmingham Railway, and the M&B, and there was considerable friction between the L&NW and the NS. This friction arose over an agreement dealing with the reciprocal arrangements for traffic over each other's lines, and the NS warned the L&NW that it had been forced to survey another outlet – a line to the Manchester, Sheffield and Lincolnshire Railway at Marple – and deed plans were deposited in 1849 to connect the Pottery line of the NS with the Whaley Branch of the MS&L, using a route which was to follow closely that of the MB&M in 1863. These plans were not pursued because, as part of the settlement with the L&NW in 1850, the NS undertook not to promote independent routes. Over the next 10 years or so, relationships between the L&NW and NS were stormy to say the least, and provided the backdrop to what later was to become a protracted and bitter dispute with the L&NW over the siting of a terminal station for the MB&M in Macclesfield.

Further along the line of the route of the MB&M, the Act incorporating the Stockport, Disley, and Whaley Bridge Railway (the SD&WB) was passed in July 1854; although this line was nominally independent, it was heavily backed by the L&NW to the extent of £299,000 out of capital of £310,000. The line from Stockport to Whaley Bridge was opened officially on 28 May 1857 and passenger services started on 9 June 1857; intermediate stations were provided at Hazel Grove, Disley and New Mills, and coal sidings were put in belonging to the Middlewood Colliery at Norbury (Middlewood); prior to that there had been a tramway connection from the colliery to the nearby Macclesfield canal.

During the period of railway development into Macclesfield and across from Stockport to Whaley Bridge, there were several abortive railway schemes, each of which would have placed Marple on the railway network. The Manchester, Buxton, Matlock, Ambergate, and Midlands Junction Railway Act of 1846 provided a line from Cheadle Hulme to Ambergate, passing very close to High Lane and the southern end of Marple; however, only the section between Rowsley and Ambergate was ever built. The Sheffield, Ashton-under-Lyne and Manchester Railway (SAM), formed in 1835, obtained parliamentary powers in 1846 to build a line from Hyde Junction via Marple to Whaley Bridge, with a branch to Hayfield; it was this line that the NS was seeking to link up with that which was mentioned earlier, and, although some construction was carried out, work stopped in November 1848 and the rails were pulled up in 1851.

From 1 January 1847, the SAM, together with the Grimsby Docks Company, the Great Grimsby & Sheffield Junction Railway, and the Sheffield & Lincolnshire Junction Railway, combined to work as the Manchester, Sheffield and Lincolnshire Railway (MS&L), and this new company was instrumental in providing the Marple area with its first railway. In 1858, the MS&L obtained parliamentary powers for a line from Hyde, via Woodley and Romiley to Compstall, the terminus being high above the Goyt Valley near Marple Aqueduct, and this opened on 5 August 1862.

Whilst construction was taking place on this line, plans were being drawn to bring another railway to Marple – in the form of the Marple, New Mills, and Hayfield Juction Railway (MNM&HJ). This was a natural extension of the line to Compstall, and, although it was an MS&L venture, it was promoted as a local enterprise in order to give it a better chance of success; included in the Act, passed on 15 May 1860, were powers for the MS&L to subscribe capital and to lease and work the line when it had been built. The L&NW was opposed to the line, since it was clearly an attempt by the MS&L to penetrate districts which the L&NW took as its own; it therefore promoted another local scheme, the Disley and Hayfield Railway (D&H), as a branch off the SD&WB. The Act incorporating the D&H was also passed in 1860 and construction began on both lines going to Hayfield. Public opinion was in favour of the Marple line and ultimately the D&H was abandoned.

From the 1840's, there were several attempts, all unsuccessful, to link Macclesfield with Warrington on the west (via Knutsford) and with Buxton on the east. For example in 1845, the Birkenhead, Lancashire and Cheshire Junction Railway, from Birkenhead to Stockport, included a branch from Warrington via Knutsford to Macclesfield. In 1860 and 1861, against the background of the Cheshire Midland Railway (CM) from Altrincham to Knutsford, the L&NW submitted a scheme linking Chelford with Knutsford by a single line 5 miles long, but withdrew it on being granted running powers to Knutsford. The CM, authorised by Parliament in 1860, became one of four lines to be operated by the MS&L and the Great Northern (GN) in 1863 as "The Cheshire Lines", and they were later joined as an equal partner by the Midland Railway (MR) in 1866. One of these lines was the 2½ mile section from Woodley to Stockport which was opened on 12 January 1863.

The MR also had its eyes on the area as part of its northern push. Buxton was its first objective, and even though the L&NW refused to let MR traffic pass through Buxton, the MR obtained powers in 1860 to construct the Rowsley and Buxton Railway (R&B). In 1861, agreement was reached between the MS&L and MR which enabled the MR to use the MNM&HJ line to reach Manchester, and this agreement underpinned the MR's Rowsley and Buxton Extension Line from Blackwell Mill (near Miller's Dale) on the R&B, to New Mills on the MNM&HJ. This was yet another rebuff to the L&NW.

This completes a summary of the pre-1863 development of the railway network in the area and provides the background for the inception and the promotion of the MB&M. The proliferation of schemes that had contributed to the railway mania of the 1840s had abated, but the intense rivalry between the L&NW on the one hand, and the MS&L and the NS on the other hand, was about to be of a totally different nature.

A print of Cross Keys public house, located in Waters Green, Macclesfield. After an arbitration case, it was eventually purchased in 1873 for £3,458, and demolished to provide better access at the front of Central station. Note the bridge in the background and a locomotive passing over. Macclesfield Express.

An 1849 print of Stoke station, headquarters of the North Staffordshire Railway – partner in the MB&M. Author's collection.

Manchester London Road station c. 1902. The headquarters of the other partner in the MB&M, the Manchester, Sheffield and Lincolnshire Railway and, after 1897, of the Great Central Railway were located in the left hand end of the building. From Great Central Railway, Volume 3, by George Dow.

2 The Line is Born - 1863 to 1864

1863 saw the promotion of the Bill which was to lead to the building of the MB&M. At that time Macclesfield was a township with a population of 40,000 people, Bollington and its surrounding area had a population of 10,000, whilst Poynton, with a population in excess of 2,000, contained Poynton Collieries, which produced 115,000 tons of coal a year, and provided a workforce, as well, for the neighbouring Adlington and Norbury collieries; Marple (including High Lane) had a population of nearly 3,400.

It was a time of depression, caused by the uncertainty and trade disruption of the American Civil War. Silk and other textile manufacturing in particular were affected, with mills closing down in Macclesfield, Bollington, and Marple. At a public meeting at Macclesfield Town Hall on 25 May 1863, a Committee of Gentlemen was formed to raise a fund to enable local silk weavers and their families to emigrate. In August 1863, 19 people, mainly families of colliers, left Poynton to emigrate to America, having received favourable news from those who had left previously. In Macclesfield alone there were 2,000 empty properties, and in recent years there had been a reduction in population of 3,000.

At a meeting of the Bollington Local Board of Health on 30 September 1863, discussion took place about the projected new railway through Bollington; much of the agitation for a new railway came in the first instance from Bollington, not at that time connected to the railway network. A committee of the board was established to watch over the Board interests of the Bollington District and this consisted in the main of well-known textile manufacturers - G. and M. Swindells, A. Greg, T. Oliver, J. Brooke and J. Gaskell.

The first newspaper reference to the MB&M appears in the *Macclesfield Courier and Herald* on 10 October 1863 which reported as follows "A line has been surveyed from Bollington to Marple, affecting a junction with the MS&L, and affording to Bollington and the important district of which it is the centre, a direct outlet to the north, and also by the Woodley Junction to Liverpool and the west, and by the Great Northern and other lines to the east. We understand that this new line, instead of stopping short at Bollington, is now proposed to be carried to join the NS . . . To the Bollington cotton spinners and manufacturers, it will afford direct and ready access to all their markets, and the extensive Kerridge stone quarries will be available over a large district where such stone is much in request. It will bring Macclesfield and Bollington into close proximity, and we are sure to participate in the advancement and prosperity which awaits the revival of the cotton trade. The Local Board of Health have appointed a committee to agree upon some plan to providing more convenient station accommodation near to Hibel Road".

The Macclesfield newspaper, the following week, confirmed that the scheme would be carried forward from Bollington to Macclesfield, and the issue of 7 November contained the following details of the line of the railway. "It commences from the NS line, near the present Macclesfield Station, and passes between Lower Heys Mill and the Lower Beech House, and thence in a nearly straight line to the Adelphi Mill at Bollington. The line crosses the Bollington road near the Wesleyan Chapel, a little on this side of the Round Gardens - and here it is proposed to fix Bollington Station, being as central and convenient as it well could be, midway between the extreme ends of the town, and about the centre of the population. It then proceeds in a direct line on the west side of the canal near the Styperson Park stone quarries, through Adlington, Pott Shrigley, Poynton, crossing High Lane to Torkington and Marple, and taking the Adlington and Poynton coal mines in its way. The line seems as straight and direct as could be well constructed, the object, we understand, being to make it a main trunk line with every facility for express trains."

Macclesfield seemed at the time in the grip of some railway fever, for not only did there appear on 14 November an advertisement promoting the MB&M, but there were also advertisements for two separate Bills promoting different railways from Macclesfield to Knutsford. The various schemes, coming forward as they did, appeared to herald a new prosperity for the Macclesfield area, with Macclesfield becoming a major centre for railway activity, and on a main east-west railway artery.

The plans of the MB&M were deposited before Parliament and at the office of the Clerk of the Peace for the County of Chester on 30 November 1863; the solicitors for the promoters were Messrs. Parrott, Colville, May & Co. of Macclesfield, with Messrs. Wyatt and Metcalfe of London, Parliamentary Agents. The length of the line was to be 10 miles, 7 furlongs, 450 links with 2 miles on level gradient and 2 miles on a gradient of 1:132 or less. The plans contained details of a viaduct 110 yards north of where the line joined the NS line at Buxton Road, and also of a viaduct at Bollington with 154 yards of arching, and with the height of the arch 25 feet and the span 30 feet. At the northern end of the line between Rose Hill and the junction at Marple Wharf, the plan showed details of a tunnel, 737 yards long. There were no details on the plans of any stations, and certainly not for Macclesfield about which there was to be so much controversy later.

The Bill contained powers for the L&NW, the MS&L, the GN, and the NS to subscribe capital to the undertaking - the sums of money likely to be needed to be well beyond the means of Thomas Oliver (a cotton manufacturer of the Waterhouse Mill, Bollington), and other local promoters. There was certainly no sign of interest from the L&NW and GN, and there was no mention of the scheme at the half-yearly meeting of the NS in February 1864. The situation was certainly different at the half yearly meeting of the MS&L in January 1864, where several shareholders expressed the view that neither the MB&M nor the other schemes emanating from Macclesfield were worthy of support. The newly appointed Chairman of the MS&L, Edward William Watkin, was uncompromising in his reply - the objectives of the MS&L were to get an independent and final footing in Liverpool by means of the Cheshire Lines, to secure a proper footing for MS&L traffic at Birkenhead, and to secure the supply of Cheshire salt which was important for the development of the ports of Grimsby and New Holland. Yes, he would bring proposals for the support of new lines before a shareholders' meeting in due course if these lines were necessary to secure MS&L's objectives.

The MB&M Bill came before the Parliamentary Committee at the end of April as an opposed Bill with 6 petitions against. One major objector was Lord Vernon, through whose lands at Poynton the line would pass, but, as a result of an agreement dated 11 May 1864, the promoters undertook to maintain and construct a siding towards Park Pit, and opposition was withdrawn. This agreement was varied under a memorandum of 12 April 1866, whereby the MB&M undertook to construct and maintain a siding of 213 yards to Anson Pit, and on 1 May 1866 Lord Vernon was paid £2,000 for purchase money for the land to be acquired, and for compensation.

During the early months of 1864 the local promoters had sought to interest the major railway companies in financing the MB&M project. Not only could they see the advantages, but so could the MS&L and the NS albeit for different reasons. The MS&L had its eyes not only on the Macclesfield and Bollington traffic, but also on the through communication to the Potteries from the Humberside ports and the South Yorkshire coalfields. For the NS, the attraction of the MB&M was control of the outlet to the north and east from Macclesfield which had the strategic advantage of reducing the dependence by the NS on the L&NW network for traffic north from Macclesfield; in the regular negotiations between the NS and the L&NW, access to the north over the L&NW metals, either via Crewe or via Manchester, was of crucial importance and the importance at that time to the NS of the MB&M cannot be underestimated, especially to prevent the L&NW getting involved.

It was these sentiments that came through very strongly at a special General Meeting of the NS held in London on 8 June. The Chairman, Thomas Brodrick, indicated the danger of the Marple line getting into 'hostile hands' as it would become another 'blockline', and stressed the need for shareholders' approval to a clause in the Bill authorising the NS and the MS&L each to subscribe £100,000; approval was given, though not without one shareholder expressing concern that this Bill, and the Silverdale, Madeley, and Drayton Bill, would delay their 5 per cent dividend.

When the Bill came before the House of Commons on 14 June 1864, the promoters were named as John Upton Gaskell, George Swindells, Edward Maisland, Thomas Wardle, Henry Brocklehurst, Edward William Watkin (MS&L), Thomas Brodrick and Lieutenant-Colonel Pearson (NS) and James Marshall; the first directors were all these gentlemen, and in addition Mr. E. C. Egerton, M.P. who had been instrumental in securing the financial support of the MS&L to the MB&M after that railway company's initial opposition to the proposals. Originally there had been six petitions against the Bill (including the L&NW) but, by the time the Bill was presented to the House of Commons, the various petitioners had withdrawn and the Bill came before the Committee on Unopposed Bills, with a change agreed between the MS&L and the NS to limit the subscription by the two companies to the building of the line to £80,000 each. This amount was later to prove to be a severe underestimate and, by the time Central station had been built and opened in 1873, total costs exceeded £430,000. Had the two companies known that the costs of building the MB&M would be as much as that, one wonders whether they would have agreed to proceed with it in the first place.

The adjourned meeting of the NS held at the London Tavern on 18 June 1864 approved the subscription powers of £80,000, though not without some critical questioning from one shareholder as to how the capital was to be raised. The same meeting also heard from the Chairman that the MS&L was making determined efforts to alter the tolls that the NS levied on its own canal, the Trent and Mersey, no doubt to the benefit of the MS&L who owned the Macclesfield canal; the NS, despite going into partnership with the MS&L in respect of the MB&M, were not prepared, on the canal issue, to yield an inch to the MS&L.

The Bill passed through the various stages in the House of Commons and House of Lords very quickly and the Macclesfield, Bollington, and Marple Railway Act received the Royal Assent on 14 July 1864. The half-yearly meetings in July and August of the MS&L and NS respectively both referred to the advantages of uniting their separate railway systems, from the Newton and Compstall branch of the MS&L at Marple to the Drayton (Market Drayton) branch of the NS.

Although the Act did not specify the precise locations of railway stations along the line, there was a strong feeling in Macclesfield that a new station should be erected between Waters Green and Commercial Road. In September 1864 there was started a strong lobby for a station on the MB&M at High Lane – previously a memorial signed by 600 people had been presented to the L&NW for a station at High Lane on the Stockport, Disley, and Whaley Bridge Railway, but had been turned down. The residents of High Lane fairly put their case – the collieries of Clayton and Brooke, and of Brocklehurst, two large cotton mills nearby, the Strines Printing Company, a National day school for two hundred scholars, a post office, brass band, and seven public houses, but no railway station!

A meeting with reference to the MB&M was held at the Queen's Hotel on 9 September 1864 at which some fundamental decisions for constructing and working the line were made; it is worth noting that this was the only meeting of the MB&M ever to take place in Macclesfield. It was agreed that the MS&L and the NS each have half the responsibility for making and working the line, and that the line be constructed and managed by a Joint Committee with four Directors each from the MS&L and the NS; in the event of dispute, the Directors had powers to select an arbitrator or to remit the selection to the Board of Trade. It was also agreed that the line be credited with its mileage of all traffic passing over it, and that each company make through rates between stations on their respective lines via the new line.

At a meeting of the Joint Committee on 17 November the matter of raising the capital to construct the line was discussed, and it was considered the best course for the two companies jointly to guarantee a fixed dividend of 5% – in doing this it was still in the minds of the Joint Committee that the MB&M should have shareholders other than the MS&L and the NS, as was permitted by the Act. It was also agreed that each company should be liable for half of any deficiency in the net receipts of the line, should meet the guarantee, and should have the right to place one half of the shares on the understanding that proper precautions were taken under existing powers and powers to be applied for, to secure the appointment of the Directors and the entire control of the undertaking.

The first General Meeting of shareholders of the MB&M took place on 15 December 1864 at the new Board-room of the MS&L, at London Road station, Manchester. The objective of the meeting was to complete the transfer of the company from the local Directors, who were the original promoters, to other Directors nominated by the MS&L and NS; the local promoters were now required to perform the duty of handing over the line to the railway companies, whose influence would be of much more service to Macclesfield and Bollington than that of a small independent company. After the meeting had agreed to reduce the number of Directors from nine to eight, the following were elected as Directors – representing the MS&L, J. Chapman, M.P., W. Fenton, E. W. Watkin, M.P. and R. Withers, and, representing the NS, Sir A. Anderson, T. Brodrick, Lieut.-Col. C. Pearson, and Col. F. W. Tomlinson.

It was also reported to the meeting that the Act prescribed that the line should be completed within five years, and that a Parliamentary Deposit of £10,400 had to be made as security for the completion of the line within that time. It was further reported that the Act gave powers to the two railway companies to take £80,000 each in shares, and to guarantee to the extent of a further £20,000 each; these powers remained unexecuted until the sanction of the shareholders was obtained – the previous approvals given by the MS&L and NS shareholders had related merely to the clauses contained in the Bill as it had passed through Parliament.

Finally, the General Meeting dealt with various appointments – J. Samuda, Secretary of the NS, and G. R. Underdown, General Manager of the MS&L, were appointed auditors, each to receive £25 per annum; the Directors were to receive £400 per annum divided as they thought fit, and the Secretary's remuneration was to be £200 per annum.

T. Wardle, on behalf of the local promoters, expressed satisfaction that there was a bona fide intention by the railway companies to proceed with the line as quickly as possible, and all present expressed their appreciation of M. L. May, the local solicitor, for all his efforts.

With the formalities behind them, the Board of the Joint Committee were now able to start the task of building the line.

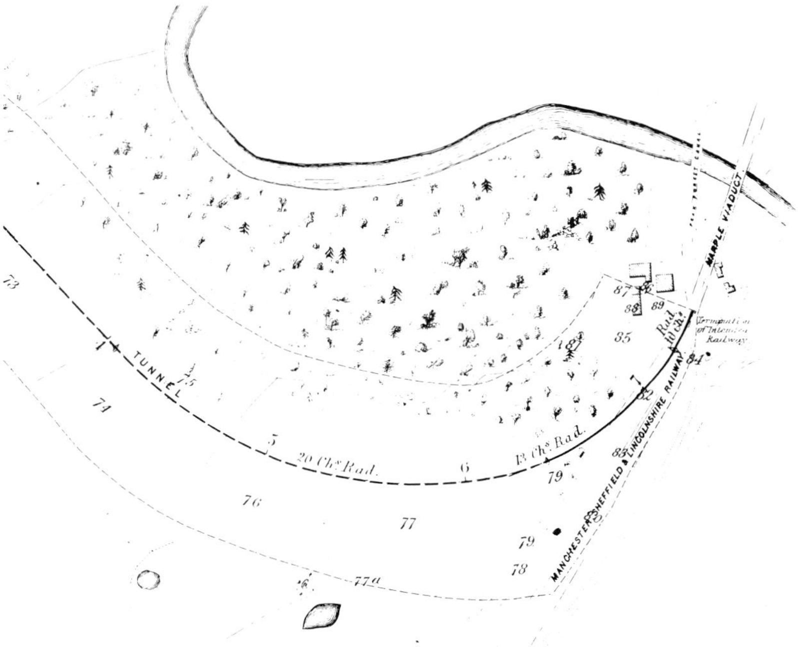

The deposited plans for the MB&M show a tunnel, 737 yards long – marked with a dotted line – located between Marple Wharf Junction and what was to become Rose Hill station. This tunnel was never built, but a deep cutting was needed instead. Note the sharp curve, 13 chains radius, where the MB&M leaves the "MS&L" line to Sheffield. Author's collection.

3 Building and Opening the Line - 1865 to 1869

A Board Meeting of the MB&M, this time held at the offices of the NS at Stoke-on-Trent, took place on 12 January 1865 - still no Chairman was appointed, though E. Ross was appointed Secretary. The issue of how to resolve disputes between the two companies 'in partnership' was again discussed, and it was agreed that no Board Meeting should be constituted without representation from each company and that no question should be carried by vote but that, in the case of differences between the representatives of the two companies, provision was made for arbitration. Messrs. Burchell and Lingard were appointed Solicitors, and Sacré and Forsyth Joint Engineers (representing the MS&L and NS respectively); each of the companies was to advance £5,200, at 5% interest per annum, to pay for the Parliamentary Deposit - a performance bond that the line would be built - and this sum was invested in 3% consols.

February 1865 saw the appropriate shareholder approvals obtained by the respective companies (i) to subscribe up to £80,000, (ii) to guarantee a dividend of up to 5% on all or any part of such capital and (iii) to the raising of additional capital under the enabling Act. At a Board Meeting on 15 February the Manchester and Salford Bank was appointed Banker, the cheque signatories being one Director of each company, and the Engineers were instructed to survey the line, and prepare land plans and plans for construction of works.

The official seal of the Macclesfield, Bollington, and Marple Railway, which was used from 1864 to 1871. Separate seals of almost identical design were used for the Macclesfield Committee from 1871 to 1907, and for the Great Central and North Staffordshire Railway Committee from 1907 to 1930. British Rail.

The Board Meeting of 12 April approved payments of £742 to Messrs. Wyatt and Metcalfe (Parliamentary Agents for the Bill), £1,605 to Messrs. Parrott, Colville and May (Solicitors to the Promoters), £1,500 to J. Mawson (for his services as Engineer), and £150 16s. to Messrs. Bradshaw and Blacklock (for preparing the Parliamentary Plans). All in all, the cost of launching the MB&M amounted to nearly £4,000.

The issue of the location of a station to serve the MB&M was raised at the Quarterly Meeting of the Macclesfield Town Council on 4 May 1865 in the context of a letter already sent by the Mayor to the Chairmen of the MS&L and of the NS in March. The Town Council offered to make all information available "with respect to the most eligible site for the intended station, keeping in view the interests of the companies and the convenience of the public . . . The present station is so obviously inconvenient in its position that the Corporation will be ready to offer any facilities of communication to a new Station which they possibly can".

At the Board Meeting of 15 June, the report of the Engineers was considered, the important features of which were that the tunnel at the Marple end could be dispensed with, and that it would be desirable to make a junction to the north of the Hibel Road station so as to use the existing station and thereby make considerable savings in outlay on land, buildings, and works; reference was made to the Parliamentary plans which contemplated an independent station to the south of Hibel Road station, and the Engineers placed strong emphasis on the railway operational difficulties of having two separate stations.

Some disquiet was expressed at the next Quarterly Meeting of the Macclesfield Town Council on 3 August about the delays in making the line and in resolving the issue of the station - all that was reported was that the line of the railway would pass on the Macclesfield, and not on the Tytherington, side of Lower Heys Mill. At the next Board Meeting on 18 October, the Engineers reported that there was no settlement of the issues relating to the site of Macclesfield station, nor of the substitution of an open cutting for the tunnel at Marple. In order to avoid further delay, the Engineers were instructed to obtain tenders from 8/10 contractors for the construction of the line, with the exception of 1 mile at Macclesfield and ½ mile at Marple, the construction of these sections to remain suspended.

November 1865 saw a meeting of the Engineers with a deputation from the Local Board of Health who expressed support for a new station between Hibel Road and Brunswick Hill, opposite the new Gas Works. A variant of this proposal came from Town Council members, who proposed an enlargement of the NS portion on the south side of Hibel Road. The Engineers reported to the Board on 24 November their dissatisfaction with this proposal, because it would involve the MB&M in the purchase, at much expense, of land and buildings over which it would have no control, and because it could involve the MB&M in having to secure further powers from Parliament - a costly process. It was the Engineers' view that a much less expensive modification to the present station could be made, and the NS had contacted the L&NW about such proposals but had not received a satisfactory reply; little were they to know that this was to be the start of several years' obstruction by the L&NW in its attempt to make the MB&M unviable.

The Board also considered the various tenders for the construction of the line, and accepted the one from Messrs. Logan and Hemingway, contractors, of Monmouth and of Altrincham respectively, in the sum of £108,482 1s. 8d., consisting of the following amounts

- excavations, including the cost of land for spoil or side cuttings and for trimming and soiling slopes	£51,845 3s. 4d.
- the maintenance of the whole line during the period of two years	£2,850 0s. 0d.
- the fencing, masonry and other works	£53,777 18s. 4d.

These and many more details were embodied in Contract No. 1, which was signed and sealed on 23 March 1866 and which was supported by a Performance Bond, of the same date, in the sum of

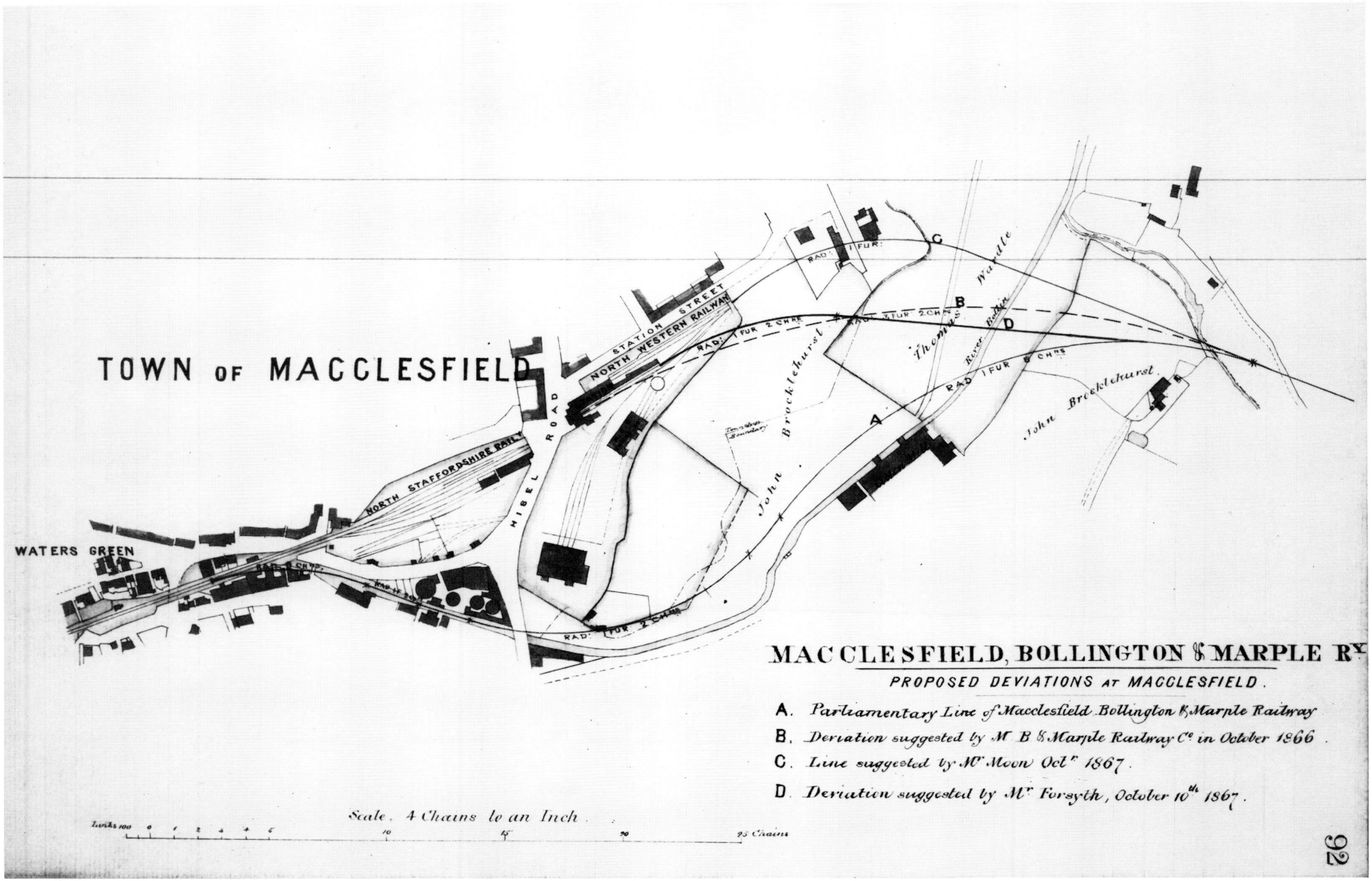

The controversy over the siting of a station in Macclesfield produced various alternative routes. This plan showing the different lines is contained in Minute Book. British Rail.

£10,900 (10% of the Contract price) binding John Logan and James Hemmingway jointly and severally for the performance of the Contract.

The Contract stipulated that the works were to be completed by 31 December 1867 with a penalty of £50 per day liquidated damages for non-completion. Clause 5 referred to the contractors' obligation to maintain the works, including the permanent way in good repair for two years after completion. Clause 22 was headed "No truck system to be allowed" and went on to say that "the contractors shall not directly or indirectly allow the sale of provisions or any other articles to any workmen employed in such works either by parties, exclusively privileged or for any other consideration than money, nor shall any control or inducement be exercised over the workmen with reference to their choice of market or to the prices for any such provision or articles. And will cause all workmen to be severally and separately paid their wages at least once a fortnight in cash on the said works and not in or within a distance of half a mile of any public house or beer shop, and that on no account shall the whole or any portion of such wages be paid or any advance made to any such workmen by tickets or orders upon victuallers or in any way whatever except in case". All this is a very interesting social commentary on the need to prevent employees from being exploited through payment in kind by their employers.

The major items of expenditure in the Contract included

33,000 linear yards of permanent fencing posts, rails	£4,125 0s. 0d.
1,310 cubic yards of excavation	£51,854 3s. 4d.
5,500 cubic yards of brickwork	£4,125 0s. 0d.
24,500 cubic yards of block and course work in mortar	£19,600 0s. 0d.
350 tons cast iron in girders, parapets	£3,500 0s. 0d.
35,000 linear yards of ballasting permanent way, single line	£4,812 10s. 0d.
35,000 linear yards laying permanent way single line	£2,187 10s. 0d.

Clause 24 referred to the intention that the line should be intended as a double line throughout, a feature of construction that becomes a subject of review later.

Reference now should be made to the other railway developments that were being proposed in the Macclesfield area at the same time, which had a direct bearing on the MB&M. On 14 November 1863, the date on which the MB&M advertisements appeared in the *Macclesfield Courier and Herald,* there were two separate Bills promoting different railways from Macclesfield to Knutsford. One was the Macclesfield and Cheshire Midland Junction Railway via Capesthorne and Chelford to Knutsford with a spur off the NS line at Sutton, and the other was the Macclesfield and Knutsford Railway via Alderley and Mobberley to Knutsford; the first of these lines was opposed and was withdrawn on 20 January 1864. There were reports in October 1863 of proposals to construct a line from Knutsford to Warrington, and although no Bill for this railway was presented for the 1863/64 Parliamentary Session, the Macclesfield and Knutsford Railway and the Knutsford and Warrington Railway Bills were presented for the 1864/65 session. It was clearly the intention of the respective promoters that the schemes should be considered as one, providing a direct link from Macclesfield to Warrington, and from there to Liverpool.

But across the Pennines, there were stirrings at the same time from the trading interests in Sheffield who were looking for a shorter route to Holyhead, an alternative route to Liverpool, and a more direct route to Buxton; during 1865 three different proposals for railway schemes from Sheffield to Liverpool were forthcoming. The one most relevant to the history of the MB&M was the Macclesfield, Buxton, and Sheffield Junction Railway (MB&SJ) whose prospectus appeared on 30 November 1865; the route of this railway was to be from Hibel Road station via Bollington, Pott Shrigley, Rainow, Kettleshulme, Whaley, Taxal and Chapel-en-le-Frith, before joining the Midland line to Sheffield; the Bill gave powers to the L&NW and the NS to subscribe.

The Board of the MB&M considered the implications of these separate developments at its meeting on 24 November 1865. The Engineers reported that both these projected railways would interfere seriously with the MB&M's construction, irrespective of any other damage, and, in the light of this, they were instructed to see whether any valid objections could be made. Criticism was also directed at M. L. May, the MB&M's solicitor, for also being the solicitor to the MB&SJ, and therefore having a conflict of interest.

The promoters of the MB&SJ sought to avoid a situation where 2 parallel railway lines (one the MB&M and one the MB&SJ) went from Macclesfield to Bollington, and so in December they wrote to the MB&M, the MS&L and the NS, about the possibility of co-operation. The major difficulty facing all railway promoters of schemes linking Macclesfield to Bollington was the steepness of the gradient between the 2 towns, and the MB&SJ plans required a continuous gradient of 1 in 70 for 5 miles in order to obtain sufficient headway to cross the Macclesfield canal in the direction of Whaley. Both the MS&L and the NS could see that the MB&SJ could damage their respective commercial interests, and indeed undermine the rationale for the MB&M, through it providing competition to the MB&M for the prospective South Yorkshire and East Coast trade, and so every effort was made to kill off this Bill. Local enthusiasm for it was sustained by the passing of the Macclesfield, Knutsford and Warrington Railway (MK&W) Act on 28 June 1866, and during July and August 1866 a series of public meetings were held in Warrington, Macclesfield, Buxton, and Sheffield, to promote the cause of the through railway. These meetings came to nought, and local interests had to be satisfied with the MK&W – this railway was never built because the promoters found difficulty in raising the necessary finance. The MK&W ceased to function after 1871, though its powers to construct a line of 11 miles between Macclesfield and Knutsford were continued in the Macclesfield and Knutsford Railway Act of 1871, the Manchester, Sheffield and Lincolnshire Railway (Additional Powers) Act of 1872, and in the Manchester, Sheffield and Lincolnshire Railway (Additional Powers) Act of 1877; the line was never built, though even as late as 1873 land was still being bought for the line.

In the meantime, in 1866 construction on the MB&M commenced and the monthly payments to Logan and Hemingway, starting in June 1866, became a regular feature; the monthly payment varied, and the 7 payments made in 1866 totalled £28,624. Reference has been made earlier to the revised agreement in March 1866 with Lord Vernon, whereby the MB&M undertook to construct a 213 yards siding to Anson Pit; in addition Lord Vernon was seeking a station to be constructed on his land near Poynton. The Bollington Board of Health was pressing the case for a suitably-sited station, but no progress was being made over the site for the Macclesfield station. There was in existence a permanent joint L&NW/NS Committee which reviewed matters of interest affecting their shared facilities and their traffic rates; at a meeting of this Committee, held at Euston on 17 October 1866, the NS, on behalf of the MB&M, presented proposals for altering Macclesfield Goods station and junction, but the L&NW objected on the grounds that it would seriously interfere with the working of its traffic. This impasse left the Board of the MB&M with no alternative but to construct the line in accordance with the Parliamentary plans (which avoided Hibel Road and passed through the Gas Works), and on 26 February 1867 the Engineers were empowered to proceed with the necessary land plans. Over the next few months, at the Macclesfield end of the line, over £20,000 was spent on purchasing land, whilst, at the Marple end, agreement had been reached with the Isherwood interests for the purchase of land at a price of £3,420, thereby enabling a deep cutting to be made north of Rose Hill, and avoiding the need to construct an expensive tunnel.

But the MB&M was facing troubles on many fronts. Firstly, there was still uncertainty about the site of the Macclesfield station and the route of the line; secondly, the Engineers had already advised the Board that the powers of compulsory purchase would expire on 14 July 1869, and that any attempt to extend the timetable for powers and for changing the Parliamentary line would be successfully opposed by the L&NW; thirdly, the economic recession was forcing the railway companies to cut back on their expansion plans. Crucial MB&M Board Meetings were held on 27 March and 15 May 1867 at which the Directors took stock of the position. The key decisions taken at these meetings were to re-open negotiations with the L&NW, and to see whether the MB&M could use the NS section of Hibel Road without the L&NW objecting; at the May meeting it was unanimously resolved "that the works on the line be suspended as far as practicable . . . and the Engineers be instructed to postpone delivery of all permanent way materials as long as possible". The financial situation was becoming so critical that the Engineers re-negotiated the conditions of contract, so that the contractors were to be paid £4,000 for May and £2,000 per month to December (provided that equivalent work had been done), the contractors were at liberty to carry out work up to £5,000 value per month, the Engineers were empowered to certify work up to that value each month, and the MB&M was to pay interest at 5% per annum from the date of the certificate on balances unpaid. The Contractors, not the shareholders, were financing the railway!!

It was, of course, too late to stop the construction of the line with so much already having been spent, but it must have been very tempting for the NS to consider this prospect at this time. On 8 June 1867, a special Shareholders' Meeting of the NS approved new working arrangements with the L&NW under a Bill which gave the L&NW running powers over the whole of the NS, with protection to local traffic, and in consideration of which the L&NW would run over the NS lines 2 fast passenger trains and 2 luggage trains daily between Manchester and London (via Macclesfield, Stoke, and Colwich), the L&NW binding the NS not to hand over at any of its termini to any other company traffic which could be carried by the 2 companies themselves. These arrangements reduced the attractions of the MB&M to the NS, as they provided an alternative (and mandatory) route to Yorkshire for traffic; this aspect was not lost on one NS shareholder, Mr. T. Oliver of Bollington, who was one of the original promoters of the MB&M, who said that the implications would be that the NS would not make use of the MB&M of which it was part owner. The rationale and viability of the MB&M was under attack even while it was being built!!

The L&NW was nothing if not a hard bargainer, and, in its approach to the route of the MB&M and to the siting of the MB&M station, it was determined to be as obstructive as possible, despite its agreement on other matters with the NS. The Joint L&NW/NS meeting at Euston on 20 September 1867 considered the matter again, and on 26 September replied with detailed proposals offering the MB&M a route into Hibel Road via a cutting into the tunnel just north of the station. The MB&M found that the total costs of this proposal (£25,000 for construction, £20,000 capital equivalent for the one-mile toll on traffic, and £2,000 for new Parliamentary powers) were greater than the costs of £40,000 for the Parliamentary line which included the expensive construction of a viaduct straddling the River Bollin; these, in any case, were too expensive, and the MB&M proposed an alternative route which avoided the tunnel but required the removal of the NS engine shed and turntable. On 1 November the NS wrote to the L&NW offering the new arrangements and on 5 November the L&NW rejected them. Despite all this, the Engineers were able to report on 9 January 1868 satisfactory progress, with works on the entire portion of the line so far advanced as to enable the contractors to begin laying permanent way from the viaduct at Bollington northwards to Norbury – a single line down the centre. But the economic depression still presented a threat to the MB&M, and the Board on 29 April 1868 requested a report on the costs of completing the line and the time-scale to enable further share and loan capital to be raised. Nine days later the Board met again and the following is a summary of the financial postion:

	Gross Amount	Paid	Estimated and unpaid
Liabilities incurred	£210,926	£107,926	£103,000
Liabilities not incurred	£51,000		£51,000

It was further reported that £15,000 could be saved if the line was made a single line, and a further report was requested on "the relative cost of making the line single or double throughout showing the cost involved if the line were made only as a mineral line . . . or as a passenger line". Before a final decision was reached on this, the Board agreed on 26 May that the line be opened as a single line as regards permanent way, the line to be worked on the system of block signalling with half a mile of double line at each of the stations; this led to the later cancellation of the contract for sleepers and the sale to the NS of rail, sleepers and chairs which were now surplus. At the same Board meeting, the tender from Logan and Hemingway was accepted for £20,000 for the completion of works at the Marple end, provided the work was completed within 12 months.

The various delays necessitated an application for an extension of time of 2 years to allow completion of works – the junction and the station and Macclesfield – and a special meeting of shareholders was arranged for 20 February 1869 to approve the application. The Engineers reported on 31 December 1868 that excavation for a proposed junction with the L&NW and for a temporary station had been completed, and that consideration should be given to the possibility of a temporary junction being formed independent of the L&NW on land owned by the NS which was situated between the joint station and the MB&M; the Engineers also suggested that the Board should dispense with the half mile of double line at the intermediate stations and adopt a single line, thereby yielding considerable savings in the working of points, crossings and signals. This led to a request for places where it was proposed to erect stations and to provide crossing places on the single line.

At the Board Meeting of 26 February 1869, the report of the Engineers was discussed and it was agreed to construct stations at Bollington, Poynton, High Lane, and Rose Hill at a cost of £500 (£650 for two platforms) and to put in a spur off the MB&M to Anson Pit at Poynton. The stations were to be small brick buildings (in fact the designs of the station buildings used on the Stoke to Market Drayton branch of the NS were used), and there was to be a single line at all stations except Poynton, which was nearest to the centre of the line, where it would be double for 440 yards; it was agreed to build dwellinghouses for station masters and porters at Poynton, High Lane, and Rose Hill (but in fact these were never built on the grounds of cost though some station accommodation was rented).

The financial situation of the MB&M had by now become serious. At 31 December 1868, the Balance Sheet total expenditure was £183,284 with the company empowered under the Act of 1864 to issue £200,000 in shares and £66,600 in loans. By June 1869 more money had been spent (£212,438) than the issued capital, and, as long as the line remained unopened, there was no chance of raising any money from outside sources. Further, both the NS and the MS&L had recently suffered loss of income from the Parliamentary reduction in canal tolls. The NS, in particular, had recently opened the line to Silverdale and Market Drayton, which was costing it £12,000 per annum in interest alone, and therefore was unwilling to to subscribe additional share capital to the MB&M if this could be avoided.

Although progress was being made towards the opening of the line to a temporary station, the major issue which was to dominate Macclesfield over the next 3 years was the route through the Gas Works, and there was to be the costly process of compensating property owners so affected. Claims from 4 landowners amounted to £7,491, though it was felt that arbitration would reduce this to £5,000; on top of this there was a likely claim of £5,000 from the Macclesfield Town Council as compensation for passing through the Gas Works, the Town fathers being torn between the choices of helping the MB&M and of securing a favourable financial settlement for the Town. One motive behind this claim was a final attempt to force the MB&M into some arrangement with the L&NW, by which a new station could be constructed south of Hibel Road and opposite the Gas Works, though Macclesfield Corporation was not anxious to have a portion of the railway line constructed above the River Bollin.

The Board met on 29 April 1869, when it was reported that a light locomotive had passed over the line. At the next meeting the Board were informed that the line would be ready for Board of Trade inspection on 1 July 1869; it was hoped to obtain sanction for passenger traffic to start on 12 July, though the line was not yet ready for goods and mineral traffic. The official inspection by Captain Tyler occurred on 23 July and was satisfactory. Also in July, approval from the Board of Trade was obtained for an extension of 2 years to complete the line. The stage was now set for the opening of the line, with many of the problems which had been facing the MB&M for several years as yet unresolved.

4 Building and Opening the station at Macclesfield - 1869 to 1873

The MB&M opened for passenger traffic on Monday 2 August 1869 from a temporary station, and over a single line of track without the link to the main line of the NS. But at least it opened. The first timetable was for 4 services a day each way between Macclesfield and Marple (Rose Hill) on weekdays and 2 each way on Sundays. 1st, 2nd and 3rd class carriages were available on each train – the fares from Macclesfield to Bollington being 4d., 3d., and 2d., respectively, to the other stations in the same proportion, and to Stockport, Manchester and Liverpool at the same rate as charged by the L&NW. The line was worked by the MS&L, "all the servants and officials wearing the uniform of that company".

MACCLESFIELD, BOLLINGTON, AND MARPLE RAILWAY.

ON MONDAY, 2nd August, the above LINE will be OPENED locally, and four Trains each way will run daily between Macclesfield and Marple (Rose Hill) Stations as under :—

Up.		Week Days.					Sundays	
		123 am	123 am	123 pm	123 pm		123 am	123 pm
Marple (Rose Hill)	dep.	8.35	10.55	3.15	6.47	...	10.35	5.35
High Lane	,,	8.43	11.3	3.23	6.55	...	10.43	5.43
Poynton	,,	8.48	11.8	3.28	7.0	...	10.48	5.48
Bollington	,,	8.58	11.18	3.38	7.10	...	10.58	5.58
Macclesfield	arr.	9.5	11.25	3.45	7.20	...	11.5	6.5

Down.		Week Days.					Sundays	
		123 am	123 am	123 pm	123 pm		123 am	123 pm
Macclesfield	dep.	7.25	9.15	2.15	5.45	...	8.30	4.10
Bollington	,,	7.32	9.21	2.22	5.52	...	8.37	4.17
Poynton	,,	7.42	9.31	2.32	6.2	...	8.47	4.27
High Lane	,,	7.47	9.35	2.37	6.7	...	8.52	4.32
Marple (Rose Hill)	arr.	7.55	9.41	2.45	6.15	...	9.0	4.40

BY ORDER.

The opening day passenger timetable advertisement appearing in the Macclesfield Courier *on 30 July 1869. The numbers above the times indicate the availability of 1st, 2nd and 3rd class travel.* Author's collection.

Although the railway companies were interested in local passenger traffic, they also made every effort to use the line to connect with their other long-distance services. The opening-day poster of the MS&L (which incidentally referred to the line as the Marple, Bollington, and Macclesfield Railway) advertised connections at Woodley for Stockport (Tiviot Dale), Warrington, and Liverpool (both for Brunswick Station and for Alexandra Buildings), Barnsley, Doncaster, Sheffield, Retford, Newark, Peterborough, London (King's Cross), Lincoln, Grimsby and Hull. At Guide Bridge, connections for Ashton (Park Parade), Stalybridge, and Oldham (Clegg Street), were advertised. All the trains from Macclesfield (New Station, as it was described) went to Manchester (London Road); the overall journey time to Manchester varied between 70 and 80 minutes and to Rose Hill between 26 and 30 minutes. From the opening of the line, "Periodical Tickets" were available from the Secretary at London Road station and from the Agents at each of the stations.

The first excursion organised was a cheap trip on Saturday 7 August to Manchester leaving Macclesfield at 2.30 p.m.; 600 people enjoyed a punctual run. The line was proving popular and, from 21 August, an additional passenger train from Macclesfield to Woodley was put on (Saturdays only for market traffic) to provide connections to Stockport, Hyde, Manchester, Ashton, Oldham and Stalybridge. From 1 September an extra train into Macclesfield from Manchester for the Saturday market traffic was also arranged.

Excursion traffic was now being arranged – the GN and MS&L ran one to London (King's Cross) on 30 August (14s. return by covered carriages) to enable people to attend the Temperance Fête at the Crystal Palace. An ambitious day out was organised by the Widows' and Orphans' Fund of the Macclesfield District of the Independent Order of Oddfellows, in conjunction with the MB&M and the Midland Railway, to visit "Baronial Haddon Hall" and "princely Chatsworth", the fare for the return journey in covered carriages from Macclesfield and Bollington being 3s. with children half price. Nearly 600 people went on the trip, the train leaving Macclesfield at 6.45 a.m., returning from Matlock at 7.15 p.m. In the first few months there were excursions by the MS&L to Doncaster Races (calling at Bollington, Poynton, and High Lane), by the NS to Trentham Gardens, and by the GN and MS&L to Smithfield Cattle Show, Islington, London (return fares, 1st class 24s. and covered carriages 14s.).

Although the line was not yet open for goods or freight traffic down to Macclesfield, this did not stop the MS&L putting on a special "coal train", starting in October 1869, from Poynton Collieries to Godley and back every day; this service only lasted for one year and thereafter coal traffic was carried by the normal MS&L goods trains. The records of the Poynton and Worth collieries show that for 1869 842 tons were sent by the Collieries' own wagons to Glossop, and that there were hopes that the new line would be advantageous in opening up coal traffic not only on the MS&L network, but also on the Midland Railway network to Hayfield, and between Marple and Buxton. Some of these hopes were realised with new customers taken on at, for example, Mottram, Northenden, Knutsford, Hayfield, Stockport (Tiviot Dale), Northwich, and Mouldsworth, and at many other stations. Despite all its difficulties the MB&M was starting to make its mark on the social and commercial life of the community. In the 5 months to 31 December 1869, 72,465 passengers were carried of which 66,541 were 3rd class with a total passenger income of £1,282 8s. 4d. Passenger train mileage in that period was 16,078 and that of goods and mineral trains 416, for which the MS&L were paid at a fixed rate of 1s. 1d. per mile; all working stock of carriages and wagons was provided by the MS&L. The operating loss for the period was £555 13s. 9d. but, after interest charges, this was increased to £1,614 2s. 8d., borne equally by the 2 railway companies.

Whilst every effort was being made to develop traffic on the line, the Board was still grappling with the financial and operational difficulties facing it; at the half-yearly meeting of the MB&M, authority was given to raise mortgages and bonds from outside sources (in accordance with the 1864 Act, in the sum of £66,600), and £8,210 had been raised by December 1869 within the powers of the Railway Securities Act 1866. This further source of money was vital for the completion of the line since both the MS&L and the NS had each subscribed the maximum under the Act, namely £100,000, and there was so much further construction to be carried out. And costs of construction were pouring in – during 1869 Logan and Hemingway were paid £36,553, McKenzie Clunes £2,350 for signalling, W. H. Dawes £6,714 for rails, and Burt Boulton £974 for sleepers.

The opening of the MB&M certainly seemed to concentrate the minds of the Macclesfield Town Council on the need to reach an early decision over the route through the Gas Works and over the amount of compensation. The *Macclesfield Courier and Herald,* in an editorial commenting on the delay in finding a solution to where the new station should be located, said "every passenger who, in the coming winter, has to get out at the temporary station, and after passing through wind, rain, snow and mud, has to wait in the old gloomy damp station for a later train to carry him to his destination will have to thank the Macclesfield Gas Committee for all the inconvenience."

On 27 August the General Purposes Committee of the Macclesfield Town Council agreed to charge the MB&M an annual rent of £100 as compensation for the separation of 2 plots of land and for the privilege of going up the River Bollin, and provided that a siding was put into the Gas Works. In the meantime the Engineers had been preparing plans for the construction of the viaduct over the Bollin and a tender was accepted in September of £5,412; the specification was amended subsequently for the viaduct to be 270 feet long, 26 feet 4 inches high, with the superstructure on cast iron columns, 12 of which were to be fixed on stone foundations in the bed of the river, at a cost of £7,272, a major amount in those days. It was the cost of the viaduct, and the other works outstanding, that led to Special Meetings being required by the NS and the MS&L in November to raise a further £20,000 each of capital to be subscribed to the MB&M.

Macclesfield (together with the question of Junctions) to the decision of an arbitrator appointed by the Board of Trade in case of non-agreement'. Even this approach was turned down.

The first 4 months of 1870 was a period of frenetic activity as everybody tried to get in on the act. On 2 February, representatives of the MS&L and the NS attended a meeting with a Ratepayers Committee, and the options of sites at Park Green and at Waters Green were considered; the Macclesfield Local Board of Health also made representations, and at a public meeting organised by the Chamber of Commerce, which took place on 16 February, a ratepayers' committee was appointed to act in concert with railway committees of the Local Board of Health and of the Chamber of Commerce. On 18 February a letter was received from E. Ross, Secretary of the MS&L, containing a suggestion from Sir Edward Watkin (General Manager) that the Mayor and the Corporation should apply immediately to the Board of Trade to appoint an Inspector who would in due course put pressure on the L&NW, and on 1 March the Mayor wrote to the President of the Board of Trade. The official enquiry of the Board of Trade, chaired by the Government Inspector, Col. Hutchinson, took place on 15 March, at which the Inspector indicated that the Board of Trade would refuse to sanction the opening of that line if the MB&M linked up

This view, reputedly 1858 but no later than 1871, is of the site of Macclesfield Central station at Waters Green before the demolition of property on both sides of the railway took place. In the foreground can be seen the railway, south of Hibel Road, and crossing Buxton Road. G. Campbell collection.

But sooner or later a decision had to be made about the siting of the station, bearing in mind that over 5 years had passed since the Act had been passed in 1864 authorising the construction of the line. On 5 October the Macclesfield Chamber of Commerce, concerned about the delay, set up a committee to confer with the Corporation about railway station accommodation in the town; the position was further complicated by the possibility of a separate station in Macclesfield for the line to Knutsford and Warrington, and by pressure from the residents of Sutton (a township a mile to the south of Macclesfield) for their own station too! The issue was aired at the next meeting of the Town Council, and there then followed an exchange of correspondence involving Messrs. Watkin (MS&L), Moon (L&NW), Pearson (NS), and one of Macclesfield's M.P.'s, W. C. Brocklehurst. A final attempt was made by the other parties to get the L&NW to agree to one station south of Hibel Road, but to no avail despite a plea that 'the Board of the MB&M are ready to leave all questions as to site, places, costs, management, and division of costs, and expenses of a new Joint Station for the three companies at

with the main line and then shunted passengers back to the existing station.

The Inspector reported on 30 March and this was ambivalent to say the least. If the companies determine to purchase fresh ground for a station, then Waters Green was the best site for general convenience; however the coal yards to the south of the station would also be convenient for the terminus of the proposed Knutsford and Warrington line; but it was 'most desirable' that the junction with the MB&M should be to the north and not to the south of the station, and the L&NW and the MB&M should reach agreement. The MB&M had by this time, given up hope of reaching an amicable settlement with the L&NW, and by the end of April Fairbairns had already completed the iron work on the viaduct over the Bollin.

Opinion seemed to be hardening locally that the most appropriate site for a station, central to Macclesfield, should be at Waters Green and the Macclesfield Town Council on 7 May recommended that this should be the location. Plans were prepared by the MB&M for the station, one on the site actually chosen and one on the other side of the Buxton Road bridge facing Commercial Road. At the MB&M Board meeting on 28 October 1870, it was reported that the L&NW

might now be disposed to reconsider an approach to a joint station, and arrangements were made for admitting the L&NW to the new station already sanctioned by the MB&M with such modifications as may be expedient; approval was then given to construct the station, if the L&NW declined, at a cost not exceeding £7,000. Next month the L&NW declined, considering it inadvisable to remove from Hibel Road, and then the MB&M approved the cost of £10,000 on the new station; on 23 February 1871 the Board, following representations from Macclesfield Corporation, agreed to the Waters Green site and not the Commercial Road site – and so, 7½ years after the Parliamentary powers were sought, the final decision was taken on the location of Central station (shown as Waters station in Ordnance Surveys of the time).

In order to ease the financial problems of the MB&M, the Board invited offers of Loans on Debenture for periods of 3, 5 or 7 years at 4½% interest per annum. This offer was successful, and by 30 June 1870 a further £19,040 had been raised, a further £30,038 was raised in the next 6 months, and, with more money raised in 1871, the total raised by Loans amounted to £66,557 12s. 4d. This sum relieved the short-term financial problems of the MB&M to the joint owners, although it all would require to be repaid within a short period of time.

A request for a station at Adlington was submitted in September 1869 by the Reverend W. J. Legh, but this was later rejected. Late 1869 and early 1870 saw the installation at Macclesfield of a water tank, warehouse cranes, a weighing machine, and the Goods station at Macclesfield opened on 1 March 1870; soon after, the MB&M became signatories to Railway Clearing House agreements for Great Britain and for Ireland. In October 1870, the Board was advised that it would cost £80,000 to complete the line, and it agreed firstly to apply to Parliament for further borrowing powers, and secondly to constitute the undertaking as the joint property of the MS&L and NS, with the requisite arrangements for managing the undertaking as a Joint Committee; these powers were secured under the Macclesfield, Bollington, and Marple Committee Act of 25 May 1871. This Act contained powers to raise additional capital of up to £60,000 from each of the MS&L and of the NS, to borrow on mortgage an amount not exceeding £33,300, and one-third of further payments made by the Macclesfield Committee (MC) on capital account. The first Board Meeting of the MC took place on 25 August 1871.

Once the decision had been made to secure the Parliamentary powers referred to above, the Board was able on 29 December 1870 to make the decision to double the line throughout. Logan and Hemingway carried out the necessary works, and tenders for the permanent way materials – rails, fish plates, chairs, bolts and nuts, and spikes – amounting in all to £9,900 were accepted in January 1871. The NS was responsible for erecting telegraphs on the line in 1871 and was paid £368; the block system was adopted as a continuation of that system on the NS line. Additional expenditure of £2,500 was authorised for extra sidings at Macclesfield.

The acquisition of land along the route was not without its problems. In March 1870, an important arbitration case, involving land at Bollington, took place at the Macclesfield Arms; the land in dispute, belonging to the Harwar family, was located on the banks of the canal near the Adelphi Mill, and was part of the Bollington Hall estate. The case was heard before Mr. J. Addison, an assessor for the sheriff, and a special sheriff's jury. Arbitration was over the damages as a result of loss of land following compulsory purchase, and the sum eventually awarded was £1,940 15s. 0d.

A more complex case arose with Mr. Antonio Arighi, a lessee from Mr. Charles Hadfield, of a silk mill at £35 per annum. Mr. Arighi had accepted compensation of £800 if suitable alternative premises could be found; the MC found that powers for compulsory purchase had lapsed in July 1871 and had not been renewed under application for extension to the Board of Trade. These powers were secured through the Manchester, Sheffield Lincolnshire Railway Company (Additional Powers) Act, 1872, but still Mr. Arighi was not satisfied. The arbitration case was heard in January 1873, the claim was for £6,105 and the jury awarded £1,650; the MC had previously offered £3,300 which had been declined. This protracted dispute delayed the opening of the new station by the best part of a year.

In addition to the construction of the new station, other construction and engineering activities were continuing. A request from Needham's Colliery at Poynton was received for siding facilities but terms could not be agreed. The viaduct over the River Bollin was passed by the Government Inspector, Lieut.-Colonel Rich, on 25 July 1871 and provided the vital link with the NS main line; Macclesfield Junction, as it was known, was 38 chains long. The double track consisted of double-headed rail, 76 lb. per yard, fixed with wooden keys, in cast iron chairs that weighed 30 lb. each; the gradient was 1 in 77. The viaduct was 317 yards long, part brick arches, with cast iron girders and part wrought iron girders over the River Bollin. In December 1871 the MC sanctioned £3,500 to be spent on goods and coal accommodation at Bollington; at the same meeting a request from William Swindells for a siding to his mill at Bollington was approved, but this does not appear to have been built.

The costs continued to mount – flood damage at Marple cost £699 in February 1873, the turntable £3,250, the engine shed £3,498, the widening of Buxton Road bridge £3,000, and the paving and metalling of the goods yards at Macclesfield £951. The balance sheet of the MC at June 1873 showed expenditure on capital account of £366,854 – almost double what was originally intended, with still further work to be done. By that date, each of the 2 companies had paid in £165,400 for the construction of the line, and borne their half share of the cumulative losses to date of £21,098. The following table shows the steady build up of traffic, particularly goods and mineral traffic, in the early years:

Half year ended	*Dec. 1870*	*June 1871*	*Dec. 1871*	*June 1872*	*Dec. 1872*	*June 1873*
Passengers	105,520	100,019	118,717	109,191	116,252	107,134
Passenger Receipts	£1,677	£1,725	£1,854	£1,807	£1,954	£1,875
Merchandise Receipts	£381	£936	£1,187	£1,711	£1,403	£2,083
Mineral Receipts	£114	£508	£703	£1,517	£1,621	£1,756
Total loss	£1,614	£4,313	£3,528	£2,535	£3,452	£1,943
Mileage:						
Passenger trains	19,818	19,303	19,929	19,385	19,957	19,236
Goods/Mineral trains	7,292	13,892	18,855	21,303	26,221	27,967

The frequency of passenger services remained unchanged in November 1870 with 4 daily each way between Macclesfield and Manchester, with an extra train each way on Saturday evening, and 3 trains each way on Sunday. All trains ran via Guide Bridge as the line via Reddish had not then been opened.

Macclesfield Junction signal box was located in the fork where the MB&M joins the NS line to Stoke just south of Hibel Road. It was built in 1872 to a standard Saxby and Farmer design, and was taken out of use in 1934. Swindells family collection.

There is very little information available about goods train services on the MB&M until the turn of the century; what does exist is contained in a series of working timetables of the Cheshire Lines Committee (CLC), which show workings from Macclesfield, but detail the timings between Woodley and the MS&L depot and exchange sidings at Godley. From 1 April 1871 there were 2 MS&L goods trains a day each way between Macclesfield and Godley, and this frequency continued until 1878. There is no evidence of any NS freight workings over the line, all NS traffic for the MS&L network and the CLC being transferred at the MC exchange sidings at Macclesfield. The importance of these exchange sidings to the NS must be emphasised as they complemented their exchange facilities at Derby (with the MR), Market Drayton (with the Great Western Railway), Burton (with the MR, L&NW and GN), and Crewe and Colwich and later Ashbourne (all with L&NW).

The early years saw the further development of passenger excursion traffic on the MB&M. On 17 February 1870, the MS&L put on a special train from London Road, calling at all stations from Rose Hill to Macclesfield, "for the convenience of persons wishing to attend the theatres, concerts, etc., at Manchester", departing at 11 p.m. with First, Second and Third class tickets available. In June 1870 "cheap Two or Three Days' excursions" were advertised by the MS&L from Macclesfield and Bollington to Grimsby and Cleethorpes, fares being 12s. return (First Class) and 6s. covered carriages; in the same month the GN and the MS&L offered "cheap Five, Eight, or Twelve Days' Excursion" to Lowestoft, Yarmouth, Cambridge, Ely, Hunstanton, Norwich, Lynn, and Wisbech by a special train on 25 July leaving Macclesfield at 9.10 a.m. and Bollington 9.15 a.m. The same companies organized a cheap excursion to the Workmen's International Exhibition at Islington in September 1870. In September 1870, also, the first annual horticultural and agricultural show took place at Macclesfield, and excursions were organized by the NS and by the MB&M. For the Macclesfield Wakes in October 1870, additional trains were put on to and from Macclesfield and Woodley (for connections), and there were excursions run from Macclesfield, Bollington and Poynton to Belle Vue Gardens (1s. 6d. including admission). On 8 December 1870 the MS&L arranged a special train for "Evening Entertainments in Manchester and Mr. Charles Hallé's Concert". These were representative of the many special excursions organised between 1870 and 1873, in addition to the regular annual excursions to, for example, the St. Leger and the Smithfield Show.

The impression is that, of the 2 partners, the MS&L were more actively promoting the excursion traffic. The NS promoted only the occasional excursion, for example in April 1870 from the Potteries to Belle Vue.

Some idea of the growth of the MB&M at Macclesfield can be measured by the report of the Railway Officials' Supper in January 1872, held at the Union Inn, of the Macclesfield and Congleton branch of the Amalgamated Society of Railway Servants which existed at that time. The 40 employees of the MB&M at Macclesfield would not only have consisted of the station master, porters, platelayers, pointsmen, and clerks, but also carters and stablehands involved with the 3 horses and carts owned by the MC.

The first 3 years had not been without friction between the MS&L and the NS. The Board were informed in August 1871 that the NS had withdrawn their freight traffic over the MB&M as a result of a dispute over rates; this issue was resolved a few weeks later. In March 1872 there was further disagreement over the use of the NS line between the junction with the MB&M (referred to as Marple Junction) and the new station. This was resolved under clause 70 of the 1872 Additional Powers Act referred to earlier, which enabled the MC and the MS&L to run their traffic, engines and carriages, free of charge over such part of the NS at Macclesfield to enable the MS&L and the MC to have free access and use of the station, booking offices, sidings, and works of the MC at Macclesfield.

The scene was now set for the next major development on the MB&M, the opening of Central station, but not before further bad luck had hit the MB&M. The new station had been inspected by Captain Tyler of the Board of Trade on 18 June 1873, the formal sanction obtained, and it was scheduled to open on 1 July. He referred to 4 lines of rail – 2 platform lines and 2 through lines – with a goods signal cabin at each end of the station "for the central concentration and interlocking of points". All this was overshadowed by a major accident at Hibel Road on 21 June, when 2 people were killed and many injured. Seven excursion trains from the Potteries had brought between 4,000 and 5,000 excursionists to Hibel Road station, which, despite recent L&NW advertisements for tenders for an enlarged station, was still inadequate and couldn't cope with the large numbers. Some excursionists crossed the tracks whilst a goods train was shunting forwards and backwards in the station, and that was that. Sadness pervaded the town when, on 1 July 1873, Central station opened for traffic.

Early excursion notices. Macclesfield Express.

GREAT NORTHERN, AND MANCHESTER, SHEFFIELD, AND LINCOLNSHIRE RAILWAYS.

SMITHFIELD CATTLE SHOW, Agricultural Hall, Islington.

A CHEAP EXCURSION TO LONDON (King's Cross Station), by the New Route, will run as under, on MONDAY, 5th December, returning from King's Cross at 11 0 a.m. on FRIDAY, 9th December.

STATIONS.	Time.	Fares to London (King's Cross) and back.	
	a.m.	cov. car.	1st clas.
Macclesfield (New Sta.)...dep.	9 10	14s.	24s.
Bollington .... ,,	9 15		

LONDON (King's Cross) arr. about 4 0 p.m.

Tickets, Bills, and every information may be had at the above Stations.

R. G. UNDERDOWN, General Manager.

London-road Station, Manchester, November, 1870.

MANCHESTER, SHEFFIELD, & LINCOLNSHIRE RAILWAY.

EVENING ENTERTAINMENTS in Manchester, and Mr. Charles Halle's Concert.

The Public is respectfully informed, that for the accomodation of parties who are desirous of attending the THEATRES, CONCERTS, &c., in Manchester, a SPECIAL TRAIN will leave MANCHESTER (London-road Station), on THURSDAY, 8th December, at 10 45 p.m., calling at the following places at the time named :—

	P.M.
MANCHESTER (London-road) ....dep.	10 45
Fairfield	10 55
Guide Bridge	11 0
Hyde Junction	11 4
Hyde	11 7
Woodley	11 12
Romiley	11 16
Rose Hill	11 20
High Lane	11 28
Poynton	11 32
Bollington	11 41
MACCLESFIELD ....arr.	11 50

Periodical and 1st, 2nd, and 3rd Class Single and Return Tickets will be available, and passengers will be booked to and from intermediate stations by this train.

R. G. UNDERDOWN, General Manager.

London-road Station, Manchester, Nov., 1870.

MANCHESTER, SHEFFIELD, & LINCOLNSHIRE RAILWAY.

MACCLESFIELD WAKES.

ON SUNDAY, Oct. 2, ADDITIONAL TRAINS, conveying 1st, 2nd, and 3rd Class Ordinary Passengers, will leave MACCLESFIELD for BOLLINGTON at 2 30 p.m. and 8 0 p.m., and Bollington for Macclesfield at 2 45 p.m. and 8 15 p.m.

On MONDAY, TUESDAY, and WEDNESDAY, 3rd, 4th, and 5th October, Additional Trains, conveying 1st, 2nd, and 3rd Class Passengers, will run between MACCLESFIELD and WOODLEY, as under :—

	p.m.		p.m.
MACCLESFIELD (New Station) ....dep.	8 15	WOODLEY ....dep.	9 5
Bollington .... ,,	8 21	Romiley .... ,,	9 10
Poynton .... ,,	8 31	Rose Hill............ ,,	9 15
High Lane .... ,,	8 35	High Lane .... ,,	9 23
Rose Hill (Marple) ,,	8 41	Poynton .... ,,	9 28
Romiley .... ,,	8 46	Bollington .... ,,	9 38
WOODLEY..........arr.	8 50	MACCLESFIELD (New Station)..........arr.	9 45

In connection with Trains to and from Manchester, Stalybridge, Ashton, Oldham, Stockport, and intermediate Stations.

On MONDAY and WEDNESDAY, 3rd and 5th October, passengers will be booked by the New Line to ASHBURYS, for BELLE VUE GARDENS, by the under mentioned trains :—

	a.m.	p.m.
MACCLESFIELD (New Station) ...dep.	10 0	2 20
Bollington .... ,,	10 7	2 25
Poynton .... ,,	10 17	2 35

Available for return from Ashburys Station, near the Gardens, at 9 5 p.m., after the Fireworks.

Fares to Ashburys and back, including Free Admission to the Gardens :—

1s. 6d., COVERED CARRIAGES.

R. G. UNDERDOWN, General Manager.

London-road Station, Manchester, Sept., 1870.

LIVER COMPLAINTS, BILE AND INDIGESTION CURED WITHOUT MERCURY.

5 The Early Years - 1873 to 1885

The new station opened on Tuesday 1 July 1873, though to no great ceremony. Nearly 10 years had elapsed since the plans were deposited and the wrangling with the L&NW, with the Corporation, and with the townspeople of Macclesfield, had gone on for years; it was with relief rather than with enthusiasm that both the MC and the town greeted the opening. The existing temporary station was to be used as stables, and, apart from a brief period in 1919 when it was used again as a temporary station during the reconstruction of the viaduct over the River Bollin, it survived in that form until it was demolished in 1947.

There was still dissatisfaction with the new station, as the *Macclesfield Courier and Herald* stated on 5 July - "though it will be a great improvement on the temporary station, it does not meet the requirements of the town or come up to the general expectations of the inhabitants". The Board of Trade Inspector had already commented adversely on the length (100 yards) of the platforms but, after much agonising, the MC rejected in February 1874 proposals for lengthening the up side but not the down side. There was general criticism, too, that the platforms were narrow and insufficiently covered, though it was agreed that the waiting rooms, porters' rooms, and booking offices on each side were very satisfactory. The construction of the new station had been achieved at the cost of a considerable demolition of property in Waters Green and Buxton Road, and a claim from the lessee of the Cross Keys public house in Waters Green, one Thomas Bayley, for loss of trade, business and leasehold interest, was settled for the costly sum of £3,458 in October 1873.

During 1873 work was completed on the new siding at Central station at a cost of £1,662, and in 1874 on the paving and other works at the goods yard at Macclesfield at a cost of £2,725. The construction of the goods warehouse at Bollington took place in the first few months of 1874 at a cost of £4,314; for some years prior to this, there had been some dissatisfaction in Bollington because the absence of such facilities meant that goods traffic had to be forwarded to Bollington not over the MB&M, but over the L&NW to Hibel Road. This extra construction had been carried out by Logan and Hemingway, who had been the contractors since their tender was accepted in 1865. They made a claim of £4,319 for loss in delay in completing the works and for loss of interest on amounts due; a settlement of £3,500 was reached and paid in December 1874. All in all, over the 9-year period Logan and Hemingway were paid £232,154, a substantial sum in those days. By December 1874 a total of £412,654 had been spent on the construction of the line, and, although some debenture loans had been used to finance the cost of construction, these were all repaid by December 1877.

In May 1874 a request was received from the Adlington Coal Company (ACC), which was owned by the Legh family, to put in a siding to connect with their colliery; previously there had been a tramway from its Kingfield Pit to the Macclesfield canal. The MC had no objection to the siding being put in, provided that ACC met the capital cost and paid for the maintenance. This was built under an agreement dated 13 November 1874 and existed for 10 years; the ACC paid for the maintenance (averaging £15 per annum) and for the costs of working the siding and signal box.

Minor works included the construction of a footpath (following the request of the Bollington Board of Health in 1874), from High Road, near the Wesleyan Chapel, to the station at a cost of £180; approval was given in 1874 to light Rose Hill station with gas; lamps for the approach road to Central station were approved in 1875 and instructions given to the Macclesfield Lighting Committee to erect them; a ticket platform to the west of Central station was approved in 1875 at a cost of £180; in 1876 approval was given to lay an additional coal siding at Macclesfield at a cost of £680.

The next major development on the MB&M was the link with the Stockport, Disley, and Whaley Bridge Railway (owned by the L&NW) at or near Middlewood (or Norbury). Reference was made in Chapter 3 to the railway Bill being promoted in 1865 to link Macclesfield, Buxton, and Sheffield and which came to nought. In August 1872 the MC considered representations, in the form of "memorials", from business interests in the north Staffordshire areas of Leek, Hanley, Newcastle, Burslem and Tunstall, and also from Congleton, Macclesfield, and Buxton, for a loop to the Disley line to be constructed at Middlewood. Without such a loop, travellers and freight from Macclesfield to Buxton would have to

The Macclesfield Committee built this locomotive shed in 1873 to house the Manchester, Sheffield and Lincolnshire Railway locomotives working the line. It was a 2-lane shed, capable of housing the normal complement of 6 locomotives. This photograph was taken two months before the shed's closure in November 1935. W. A. Camwell.

The "lower" Middlewood station c. 1905, looking towards Hazel Grove. The bridge carried the MB&M between Middlewood and High Lane. Through the trees on the left can be seen the original signal box to Knotty design, built on the opening of the two stations in 1879, and taken out of use in 1885 on the opening of the Middlewood curve. It remained in use as a hut until at least the 1920's. Author's collection.

travel north to Stockport to change for Buxton; a loop at Disley would reduce the rail journey from 31 miles to 20 miles. The scheme had the support of the NS, the MS&L raised no objections, the L&NW were non-committal but refused to give undertakings that they would not oppose a Bill going through Parliament; the landowners on the loop, Mr. Legh, M.P., of Lyme Hall, and Lord Vernon, both consented.

This particular scheme was not proceeded with, but it was raised again at a Board meeting of the MC in May 1877 where the advantages to passengers from north Staffordshire were again repeated. It was reported that the L&NW was unlikely to grant running powers over its line from Disley to Buxton on terms favourable to the MC. The matter was further considered in August 1877 by the Board, where the ingenious suggestion was put forward of extending the platform at Poynton and of putting down steps to the L&NW line, in order to achieve an exchange of passenger traffic without inconvenience and at small cost. In March 1878, it was agreed to build an exchange station at Norbury as part of a complementary arrangement which provided for the L&NW to build its own station at Norbury; the cost of the station, built by John Bustard, was £1,323, the signal box, built by McKenzie and Holland £661, and the footpath between the stations £39. The new stations were opened on 1 April 1879 and improved passenger services, involving the co-ordination of respective timetables, were introduced on 1 June 1879.

This proved to be only a partial and temporary solution to the encouragement of traffic between Macclesfield and Buxton, both passenger and freight. June 1882 saw the first discussion of what was later to become the link between the two lines, the Middlewood curve; the NS still supported the link but the MS&L, unable to secure reciprocal arrangements with the L&NW, refused to pay for the construction of the line but would not oppose any legislation. On 6 November 1884, at a meeting of the Chairmen of the L&NW and of the NS, it was agreed that the L&NW should arrange for the land purchase and for works to be commenced using powers which were earlier obtained under the London and North Western Railway (Middlewood Junctions) Act of 28 July 1884. It was arranged at the same meeting that, on the opening of the curve, the NS should run certain trains to be agreed on in connection with L&NW express trains through from Macclesfield to Buxton on the same terms as between Macclesfield and Manchester; it was agreed that the L&NW should bear the cost of working and maintaining the junction at the Buxton end of the curve, the NS at the Macclesfield end, and the remainder of the curve to be maintained by the L&NW at joint expense. The cost to the MC of this development was £404 for putting in the junction, whilst McKenzie and Holland were paid £396 for signal work; the original signal box at Middlewood, put in when the station opened in 1879, was taken out of use and remained disused at least until the 1920s. The curve opened on Tuesday 26 May 1885 but more of that later.

There were other engineering developments between 1873 and 1885. In 1878 Messrs. Clayton and Brooke, who worked the Norbury Colliery which was owned by Lord Newton, requested a siding under an agreement made while the MB&M Bill was passing through Parliament in 1864, although they now wanted a siding on a

The starter signal of NS design, at Middlewood Higher on 9 March 1952, looking towards High Lane. Note the width of level ground beyond the track on the up side, which in the late 1870's and 1880's contained sidings for Clayton and Brooke's colliery at Norbury. Beyond the signal on the right hand side can be seen the cutting and incline which took the railway over the nearest of the two bridges towards the colliery. N. R. Knight.

different site from that contemplated in the agreement. The cost of the sidings and interlocking signals amounted to £910 of which the Colliery was to pay £490; the siding was taken out in 1892 when the Colliery closed. Extra accommodation for cattle traffic at Macclesfield was approved at a cost of £600.

In October 1883, the Marple Local Board requested a goods siding at Rose Hill station and this was approved by the MC in April 1884 at a cost of £537; a weighing machine was also installed at a cost of £100. At Bollington, lamps were installed in 1884 from the station to Wellington Street.

Between 1873 and 1885 there was the steady expansion of passenger services; passenger train mileage for the half year to December 1873 amounted to 24,499 and for the corresponding half year in 1878 was 29,888. No further details are available but locomotive expenses (payable to the MS&L – there was scarcely any NS working over the line) in the December 1873 half year was £4,139, in the corresponding half year in 1878 was £2,976, and in 1884 was £2,944; from April 1874 the rate per mile payable to the MS&L was 1s. 2d.

The October 1875 passenger timetable shows 5 daily services from Central station to London Road (3 via Guide Bridge and 2 via Bredbury) with the fastest journey time via Guide Bridge being 65 minutes and via Bredbury 45 minutes; in addition there was a daily service from Central to Hyde and a Saturdays only service, at 8.15 p.m., to London Road. Between London Road and Central there were 3 trains each via Guide Bridge and via Bredbury, the fastest journey times being 63 minutes and 50 minutes respectively, as well as the Saturday evening slow; there were 3 trains each way on Sundays. Even this level of service did not satisfy contract holders, and they petitioned the MC for improved services.

The NS passenger timetables for 1882 show 6 trains a day each way and 4 on Sunday, between Central and London Road. On weekdays there were reasonable connections with the Churnet Valley line to and from Leek, Derby, and Burton and with the main line to and from Stoke, Stone, and Stafford as far as the NS was concerned, and via Romiley to and from Stockport (Tiviot Dale), Warrington (Central) and Liverpool (Central), as far as the CLC was concerned. In addition to the Saturday evening "slow" each way, there was a daily "shuttle" each way between Central and Bollington (a 7 minute journey time), 8.15 p.m. (Saturdays excepted) and 10.15 p.m. (Saturdays only) from Macclesfield with the respective return workings at 8.30 p.m. and 10.30 p.m.; the late night Saturday workings from Macclesfield were intended to serve those enjoying themselves in Macclesfield.

Excursions between 1873 and 1885 provide some very interesting information, not only to show how the railways provided the opportunities for people to travel, but also how the different railway companies used each other's networks to move passengers. May 1875 saw the MS&L provide a day excursion for the Chester Cup Day from Macclesfield Central (leaving at 9.10 a.m. and returning from the New Northgate Station at 6.45 p.m.), 10s. 0d. first class and 5s. 0d. covered carriages; a similar excursion was arranged in May 1878. These particular excursions replaced the long-standing NS excursions to the Chester Cup via Stoke and Crewe.

June 1, 2, and 3 1882 saw collaboration between the MS&L and the NS on an excursion working via the MB&M, and there were many more such workings during 1882. These June excursions were from Manchester (London Road) to Ashbourne, worked by an MS&L locomotive throughout with an NS pilot from Macclesfield. Collaboration between the two companies was such that, for the August bank holiday, the NS lent 20 carriages to the MS&L at Macclesfield. On 5 August the NS organised an excursion from Stoke to Liverpool (via Endon and Leek, and over the MB&M – hardly the most direct route) with an NS locomotive, MS&L stock, and an NS guard. On 8, 9 and 10 August there were excursions from Stoke to Belle Vue via the MB&M with an NS locomotive

A view of Middlewood station, just before closure in November 1960, looking towards the Pennines. Middlewood was of different design to the other MB&M stations, having been built in 1879, some 10 years after the other stations, as an exchange station with the Middlewood station on the L&NW line between Stockport and Buxton. R. Hughes.

throughout and an MS&L pilot. On 15 August there was an excursion between Oldham Central and Trentham, via the MB&M, using an NS pilot from Macclesfield, and similar arrangements were made for a Manchester (London Road) to Alton Towers excursion on 28 August; for the MS&L excursion from London Road to Birmingham (Curzon Street) via the MB&M, an NS engine was used throughout.

In 1882, cheap weekend excursions were available throughout the summer from the Potteries to Buxton, via Macclesfield and Middlewood, every Friday and Saturday with the return journey on Monday or Tuesday; the first class return from Stoke was 8s. 0d. and the third class 4s. 0d.; similar arrangements applied in 1883.

February 1883 saw 2 separate excursions from Stoke, via the Loop line and the MB&M, to Manchester (Central), and Blythe Bridge/Uttoxeter via the MB&M to Manchester (Central). In the summer of 1883, excursions over the MB&M were from Bollington to Leek, Oldham and Stalybridge to Ashbourne, Bollington to Buxton (change at Middlewood), Rose Hill to Birkenhead (via Harecastle), Guide Bridge to Alton Towers, London Road to Trentham, and Bollington to Birkenhead (again via Harecastle). Not to be outdone, the L&NW provided excursions in 1883 from Buxton (change at Middlewood) for Rudyard, Leek, Oakamoor and Ashbourne. The MS&L excursions from London Road to Alton Towers continued in the summer of 1884.

But passenger travel was not without mishaps and accidents. The first occurred on 1 November 1875 at Bollington in which one man was killed and two were injured, when the 7.40 p.m. "Woodley Goods" from Macclesfield collided with a furniture wagon which had become detached during shunting at Bollington; the engine was derailed at the viaduct and the driver, a Mr. Champion Lunn, who was at the tender end (the locomotive was working tender first) was killed instantly.

A second accident occurred on 5 June 1882 at Macclesfield (Central) station when the 8.48 a.m. North Staffordshire train from North Rode was at the ticket platform when it was run into by an empty MS&L train travelling at a fair speed; among the injured was the Reverend McAulay, a Wesleyan minister from Congleton, who claimed for damages. This produced a dispute between the MS&L and the MC as to the liability for the accident, with Edward Watkin, the Chairman of the MS&L, claiming that the price paid to the MS&L for locomotive power and carriage stock did not cover claims arising from accidents; the MS&L felt that the costs should be borne by the MC, under arrangements similar to those with other joint lines, such as the CLC and the Sheffield and Midland line. McAulay received £400 from the MC, whilst costs, medical fees and legal expenses amounted to £454; the cost to the MC was very substantial in relation to its annual losses.

The period between 1873 and 1885 was less than satisfactory for goods and mineral traffic, and train mileage declined from 29,158 in the half year to December 1873 to 23,181 in the corresponding half year in 1878; this decline almost exactly balanced the increase in passenger train mileage. In April 1878, the frequency of goods trains increased, 3 a day each way Tuesdays to Saturdays, 2 each way on Sundays, and 1 each way on Mondays; this pattern of service remained unchanged until 1883 at least. The early MB&M success in attracting coal traffic from Poynton Collieries on to the MS&L network was not sustained, and coal to Bollington still came in the main by canal; in 1880, 78 tons came by rail to Bollington whilst 1,744 tons came by canal and all from Anson Pit, the pit located nearest to the MB&M and to the Macclesfield canal. Small amounts of coal in 1885 went to Bollington, Rose Hill, and Middlewood stations, the transit rates being charged were 9d., 9d. and 6d. respectively, on a selling price of coal of 8s. 5⅛d per ton. The Adlington Coal Company were successful in the tender for the coal contract from the Bollington Local Board for 500 tons of gas coal (at 7s. 6d. per ton) in 1880, 1,000 tons in 1881, and 1,000 tons in 1882; also coming by rail was 3,000 tons of cannel in 1882 for the Bollington Gas Works.

In 1879 the NS used the exchange sidings for the following traffic – goods traffic to and from Burton, Colwich and the Stoke area, goods and mineral traffic from Tutbury, and salt traffic from Wheelock (near Sandbach).

In the early 1880s, the rental agreements for the coal sidings at the MC goods yard show as tenants (in truck lengths) the Macclesfield Gas Company 24, the Macclesfield Equitable Provident Society 6, and 8 different local coal merchants a further 57.

Receipts from merchandise and mineral traffic in the half year to December 1873 amounted to £2,314 and this built up to £4,936 in the corresponding half year to December 1878; this level remained constant to 1885. Over a similar period receipts from parcels, horses, and carriage traffic increased from £203 to £851 but this level declined from 1881 to a stable level around £435 per half year by 1885. Receipts for conveying livestock never exceeded £83 in any half year and such traffic was therefore very light.

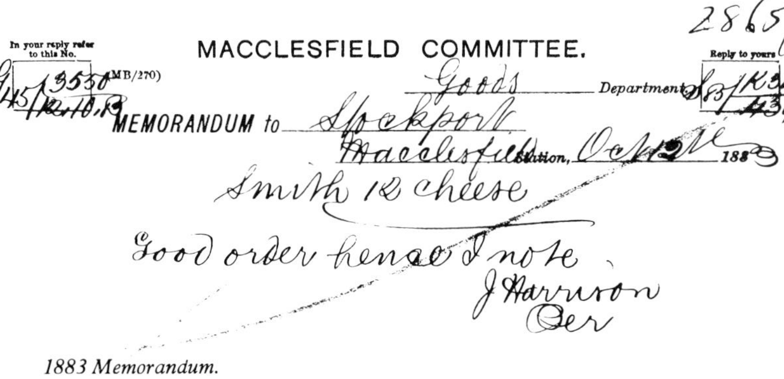
28657
In your reply refer to this No. (MB/270)
MACCLESFIELD COMMITTEE.
Goods Department
Reply to yours
MEMORANDUM to Stockport
Macclesfield Station, Oct 12th 1883
Smith 12 cheese
Good order hence I note
J Harrison
Per

1883 Memorandum.

No details survive of the number employed by the MC, but, taking the size of wage bill as a measure, it increased from £1,182 per half year in December 1873 to £1,723 in December 1878, before it stabilized around £1,800 per half year through to 1885.

And so this era of the MB&M ends, immediately prior to the opening of the Middlewood curve, a development which was, for a while, to boost its fortunes. This was clearly needed because, in the preceding 23 half years of trading, losses had been sustained in 20 of them, yielding a net loss over the period of £24,350.

6 Expansion and Prosperity - 1885 to 1907

The construction of the Middlewood curve took place during the early part of 1885 and, when the Board of Trade Inspector visited the site on 20 May 1885, he found the flyover substantially and carefully constructed with the steel girders sufficiently strong. Because the different railway companies had been unable to reach agreement as to what instruments should be placed in the Middlewood Low and High Level Junction cabins - the L&NW wanted a Tyers instrument with a single wire, whilst the MS&L wanted a three-wire system - he felt it essential that the same system be adopted in both cabins before he could sanction the opening up for passenger traffic.

In the event, the curve opened on 26 May 1885 and consisted of a "flying juction" carrying a single line over the L&NW line before connecting with the line to Buxton, with a line and exchange sidings linking the line from Buxton to the MB&M to Macclesfield. The first train to travel over it was an excursion from Birmingham, Wolverhampton, and the Potteries to Buxton. This train, which consisted of 14 coaches and was heavily laden, left Birmingham at 8 a.m., Stoke at 9.35 a.m., and arrived at Buxton a few minutes after 11 a.m., thus covering a distance of 83 miles in 3 hours. The initial passenger services to Buxton from Macclesfield Central was the 10.40 a.m., connecting with the 9.50 a.m. from Stoke, and the 9.05 a.m. from Uttoxeter, and the 3.45 p.m. connecting with the 3.11 p.m. from Stoke. There was a through express train from Buxton at 11.45 a.m. for Macclesfield to connect with the 12.36 p.m. to Stoke, and a 5 p.m. from Buxton to connect with the 5.49 p.m. Macclesfield to Stoke. The overall journey time each way was 40 minutes, and the construction of the flyover was intended to encourage through express workings. The service was increased to 3 trains each way in July, August and September.

Bollington station c. 1905 looking south. In the background can be seen the extensive goods yard and sheds, and the tall signal box. The station building plans for the NS line from Stoke to Market Drayton, which was constructed at the same time as the MB&M, were used for Bollington, Poynton, High Lane, and Rose Hill stations. Author's collection.

The period from 1885 until 1907 saw no great construction activities of significance. It was agreed in 1886 to spend £200 for stables at Bollington. In August 1888, representations were received from Lord Vernon concerning the MC's obligation under the agreements made in 1864 and in 1866, when the Parliamentary Bill was being promoted. The background to these representations was that the output of the Park Pits had been increased greatly during 1885-86 by the sinking of a new deep shaft, and by 1888 Princes Incline and Park Incline were unable to handle wagons as rapidly as required. A new plan was thus evolved to convert Princes Incline to

Middlewood
1890

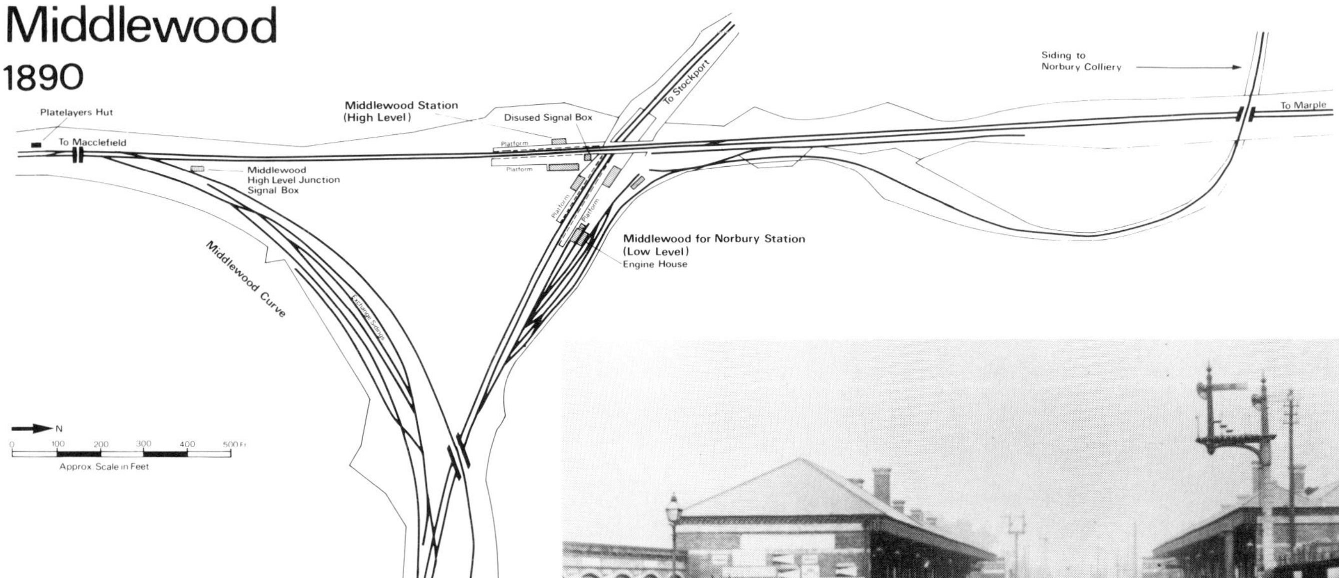

A view of Macclesfield Central station, c. 1896, facing north. On the far right can just be seen the brickwork of the Central South signal box. On the right can be seen signals of a standard NS design. Beneath the signals can be seen the water column at the end of the platform, and behind the fencing on the right are the sidings of John Potts, one of Macclesfield's coal merchants. British Rail.

locomotive haulage and to abandon Park Incline. The branch to Anson Pit was built and opened in 1869 but the projected line direct to the top of Park Incline was never built; the new extensions at Park Pits revived the matter and the Colliery Management presented a new scheme. The MC recognised its obligation as binding, but was also aware that the new siding would enable considerable traffic to be secured from the colliery at the expense of the L&NW. The total cost of the new line to Anson Pit and other alterations amounted to £4,461, which included £1,180 for the new locomotive, Lady Bulkeley, an 0–6–0 Tank built by Kitsons, and the MC agreed on 26 August 1888 to contribute £3,000; it was settled that the MS&L and the NS contribute £1,500 each. A new single track was built on a fairly level course from Park Pits direct to Anson Pit, via Quarry Pit, and was opened on 11 February 1889.

In 1887, a siding for J. & M Tymm was put in at Rose Hill. In 1890, there was increased siding provision (£530) and a new waiting room (£236) at Rose Hill, whilst the adoption of the block system of signalling to comply with Board of Trade requirements cost a further £133; also in 1890, the platform at Poynton station was lengthened at a cost of £162. In 1892, approval was given to build a station master's house at Middlewood and the tender from Thomas Yoxall of Stoke for £260 was accepted; this was the only house built by the MC anywhere on the line. In November 1892, after it was announced that the MS&L were ceasing to be carriers on the Macclesfield canal, it was agreed that increased goods accommodation at Bollington was needed to cope with the extra traffic that would in consequence fall on the MB&M; a sum of £1,800 was approved. From 1893, the Buxton Lime Firm Company had a siding at Rose Hill and this arrangement continued until 1928. Proposals came forward in 1895 for a central L&NW, MS&L and NS station at Macclesfield, but agreement of all 3 companies was not forthcoming. In November 1897, it was agreed to provide fire appliances at all stations (except Bollington where water would be taken from the canal) at a cost of £112.

1899 saw improvements in facilities right down the line. At Macclesfield, for £570, additional warehousing, a small crane, sett paving, and an extra siding was provided. Extensions were approved to obviate trains overlapping the platforms and to improve greatly the working of traffic. At Rose Hill, the up platform was extended and a cross-over road provided for £326; at High Lane and Middlewood, the up platforms were extended at costs of £85 and

In 1900, a stage was provided at the Macclesfield goods warehouse for the storage of grain for the Hovis Bread Flour Company Limited. Because of the growth of traffic at Bollington, which resulted in an increase in cartage staff, the existing stables were inadequate and £230 was approved for additional stabling.

In February 1903 the Board received reports on 2 Parliamentary Bills. The first, the North Western Electricity and Power Gas Bill contained proposals, firstly to acquire land at Bollington between the railway line and the canal on which to build a generating station and, secondly, to break up streets which would interfere with MC property; this Bill was later incorporated into a wide Bill, introduced in the 1903/04 Parliamentary Session as the Cheshire Electricity Power and Gas Bill but was rejected by a Committee of the House of Commons in the spring of 1904.

The second Bill referred to was the Macclesfield and District Electric Tramways Bill, which contained proposals to construct a nearly 20 miles system of electric tramways from Macclesfield to Hazel Grove with branches planned to Prestbury, Bollington and Sutton. This Bill was a potential threat to the MB&M because it sought to carry animals and goods as well as passengers; it was intended to cross the line of the MC with a tramway whilst at Hibel Road it would also affect the entrance to the joint L&NW/NS goods station. This Bill, too, was withdrawn because the promoters faced major difficulties with Macclesfield Corporation. This Bill was re-presented in 1903/04 Session as the Mid-Cheshire Tramways Bill but was later withdrawn.

A further Bill that the MC considered was The High Peak District Light Railways Bill, presented to the Light Railway Commission in November 1902, which had the ingenious plan of placing a railway down the middle of the main road between Macclesfield and Buxton, via the Cat and Fiddle. These proposals would have cost £85,696, but in view of the strong opposition to these plans from the citizens of Buxton, who objected to the implications from this scheme of smoke polluting their genteel streets, were never seriously considered.

There is no doubt that, had the Tramways and the Light Railways schemes secured Parliamentary approval, they would have taken away a lot of local passenger traffic between Macclesfield and Poynton on the one hand, and Buxton on the other hand. Some

A view of Macclesfield Central station looking south, c. 1897. Beneath the water tower can just be seen the top of the original Central South signal box. In the foreground can be seen the cattle pens. Swindells family collection.

Alterations at the turn of the century to the Mortar Mill sidings of John Potts, led to the re-siting of the water tower and the replacement of the original signal box with a new signal box, seen here to the right of the water tower. This box is of a later NS design. Bullock family collection.

A view of railway activity at Macclesfield at the turn of the century. In the foreground can be seen the roof of the NS engine shed at Hibel Road and to the left can just be seen a NS DX Class 0–6–2T. Note the fence which separates NS and L&NW activities from those of the MB&M. Beyond the fence on the left can be seen the original (1869–73) MB&M station, used as stables until the late 1930's and as a garage until 1947. Behind the station on the far left can be seen the end of the goods shed. The extensive coal sidings can be clearly seen and beyond are the running line to Bollington and the exchange sidings. G. Fox collection.

MS&L 2-4-2T, F1 Class, 574, seen here working a passenger train to Manchester across the bridge over the Buxton Road at Macclesfield, c. 1893. This locomotive was built in June 1889, and was the first of this Class which lasted down to 1949. In the bunker can be seen some wood, and behind the engine can be seen the wooden ticket platform. Author's collection.

years earlier there had been local discontent expressed at a meeting of the Bollington Urban District Council when, in November 1896, proposals came forward for the Macclesfield and Leek Railway, which was part of a much larger scheme linking Derby and Nottingham with Manchester, via Leek, Macclesfield, Prestbury, Wilmslow and Styal, and linking up with the CLC at Baguley. The view of the Urban District Council was that the MB&M train service was wretched, and that every effort should be made to get the Macclesfield and Leek Railway nearer to Bollington. The scheme, however, foundered because of lack of financial support from Macclesfield.

In October 1904, the MC approved additional sidings to be installed at Rose Hill for £1,186, which would considerably relieve the working and would increase the coal business. In May 1906 it was agreed to re-lay 3¼ miles of permanent way, the costs to be charged out at half a mile a year; this amounted to £4,073 and it was later agreed to charge it at £600 per half year.

In 1897, the MS&L changed its name, by the Great Central Railway Act of that year, to the Great Central Railway (GC) because, with the forthcoming opening of the "London extension", a more appropriate name was needed. Because of this change of name, it was subsequently necessary to change the titles of some of the joint committees; under Clause 112 of the Great Central Railway Act of 1907 the Macclesfield Committee ceased to exist, to be replaced by the Great Central and North Staffordshire Railway Committee (GC/NS), and this date is a convenient break point in the history of the MB&M.

The development of passenger services on the MB&M falls into 2 parts during this period – the first part deals with the services between Macclesfield (Central) and Manchester (London Road) described in the MS&L passenger timetable as "between Manchester, Marple, Bollington, and Macclesfield" and the second part with the services between Macclesfield and Buxton described in the NS passenger timetable as "Manchester, Buxton, Bollington, and Macclesfield".

In August 1887 there were 7 trains a day from Macclesfield to Manchester of which 3 were all stations via Bredbury, 2 were for stations to Romiley and then Ardwick only, 1 all stations via Guide Bridge, 1 all stations to Guide Bridge and then to Manchester, stopping at Ashbury's (for Belle Vue) on Saturdays when required. The fastest journey time to Manchester was 47 minutes on the 9 a.m. all stations to Rose Hill, and then Romiley and Ardwick only, obviously the businessmen's special. There was an early afternoon train each way between Macclesfield and Bollington, on Saturdays only for the Macclesfield market trade, and this service was strengthened by making Bollington a stop on the express services between Macclesfield and Buxton. On Sundays there were 4 trains

NS locomotive, 2-4-0, Class C, "Colin Minton Campbell", seen here at Macclesfield on the through down line, c. 1902. It was one of only two NS locomotives to carry names after 1870. L.C.G.B. Ken Nunn collection.

from Central to London Road, all stations via Guide Bridge, but none called at Middlewood.

Between Manchester and Macclesfield there were 5 trains daily. There was a Saturdays only train from Manchester (for businessmen mainly) at 1.30 p.m. calling at Ardwick, Bredbury and Romiley and then all stations to Macclesfield, another Saturdays only train from Woodley (with connections from Manchester) at 11 p.m. arriving at Macclesfield 11.35 p.m. to cope with passengers who had enjoyed an evening out in Manchester. The 4.20 p.m. calling at Ardwick, Bredbury, and Romiley and all stations to Macclesfield (journey time 48 minutes) was a businessmen's train which did not run on Saturday. The Bollington-Macclesfield service had the extra

Saturday afternoon journey, being the return working of the market special, and was strengthened by the stop on the Buxton to Macclesfield expresses. Of the 4 Sunday trains, 3 were all stations via Guide Bridge, and the fourth, Ardwick, Guide Bridge, and then all stations to Macclesfield; again none stopped at Middlewood.

In addition to the through services from Macclesfield (Central) to Manchester (London Road), the MB&M provided an important link between the NS network to the south and the MS&L and CLC networks both west and east of Manchester. For example, in August 1887 the 9 a.m., 10.50 a.m., 1.40 p.m., and 4.10 p.m. trains from Macclesfield had booked connections from NS lines from Burton,

GCR 2-4-2T, F2 Class, being given the right of way at Mortar Mill, Macclesfield for shunting duties, c. 1905. Behind the wooden fencing can be seen the sidings of John Potts & Co., local coal merchants, and various private owner wagons. On the right of the picture can be seen a ground signal of standard NS design. Manifold collection.

Derby, Uttoxeter, Stone, and Stoke, and to Warrington (Central) and Liverpool (Central); the journey time from Macclesfield to Liverpool was 1 hour 50 minutes. Some of the connections involved long waits; passengers from Stoke had to transfer from Hibel Road and wait nearly 2 hours for the 1.40 p.m. In the reverse direction, the 10.35 a.m. and 4.20 p.m. from Manchester (London Road) to Macclesfield (Central) provided similar connections from Liverpool, Southport (Lord Street) and Warrington to the NS network; in this case the delay at Macclesfield was 56 minutes and involved a transfer from Central to Hibel Road in respect of the 4.20 p.m.

By summer 1903, the passenger service had been strengthened so that there were 8 trains daily, 1 extra on Saturdays only, and 5 on Sundays; the first train in the morning was the 6.55 a.m. which enabled working people to get to Bollington, Poynton and beyond; it was more difficult for working people from Poynton and Bollington to get to the Macclesfield mills early – the first train was 8.26 a.m. from Poynton and 8.34 a.m. from Bollington. From Manchester to Macclesfield there were 7 trains daily, 1 Saturdays excepted, and 1 Saturdays only and 5 on Sundays; in addition, there was a London Road to Rose Hill train (Saturdays excepted) for businessmen at 5.52 p.m. which worked back at 6.48 p.m.

The Macclesfield to Buxton service between 1885 and 1907 was subject to many variations, and its importance to the L&NW diminished following the opening of the L&NW line from Ashbourne to Buxton in 1899. The inaugural service in 1885 was 2 trains a day each way on weekdays, with an extra service each way from July to September; for August and September there was a 7.35 p.m. train from Buxton to Macclesfield. The winter 1885 service reverted to 2 trains a day each way, but this was suspended from 1 January to 19 April 1886, when the two-train service was reintroduced. The "New Express Route to Buxton", as it was known, was promoted by the L&NW, the MB&M, and the NS, and was aimed at the London/Birmingham passenger to Buxton. London through carriages to Buxton were advertised, travelling via Stafford and the NS, in the summer of 1886, but after October 1886 these coaches were suspended and the connection was made with the noon Euston express to Hibel Road. The afternoon express Buxton train on the MB&M was started back at Hibel Road at 3.50 p.m. and this became normal practice in succeeding years. From 1887 to 1889 the July/August/September service from Macclesfield (Central) connecting with the noon Euston express was at 4.05 p.m. arriving at Buxton at 4.45 p.m.; this also connected with the 2.56 p.m. from Stafford via Stoke. The London to Buxton services, outside of the summer months, also ran in May, June, and October in 1887 and 1888, and in June and October in 1889; the train was 10 minutes earlier in those months at 3.55 p.m. with no connection from Stafford. Until 1890, through carriages were provided from Stafford to Buxton, whilst passengers off the noon Euston express changed at Hibel Road to join the Buxton train which left Hibel Road at 3.50 p.m., with the carriages worked through to Central for the journey to Buxton. After 1890 the through passengers, if any, had to make their own way from Hibel Road to Central – with a pretty small margin of time! The ambitions of the London to Buxton route, via the MB&M, were shortlived.

The general pattern of service through to Buxton between 1891 and 1899 was basically constant; a daily service, from 1 July to 30 September, of 3 trains each way with extra trains on Mondays and Saturdays. The connecting services from the NS network (10.40 a.m. at Central from Stoke and 10.34 a.m. from the Churnet Valley) linked with the 10.45 a.m. to Buxton (stopping only at Bollington) and the 10.50 a.m. down the MB&M to Manchester (London Road). The connecting services for the 3.55 p.m. and the 7.50 p.m. to Buxton were less satisfactory, involving a change of trains at Hibel Road. The journey time to Buxton was 40 minutes and from Buxton between 38 and 41 minutes.

Between 1900 and 1904, the frequency of service was reduced, twice daily each way and an extra service on Saturdays until 1905; trains were run July to September during this period. From June to August in 1905 to 1907, the service was contracted further with 2 trains each way on Mondays, Thursdays and Saturdays only, and an extra train on Saturdays.

The MS&L "Programme of Tourist and Continental Arrangements" for November 1891 provides interesting details of season tickets facilities, which were available for 3, 6 and 12 months for 1st, 2nd and 3rd class travel. Such facilities were available between Manchester (London Road) and between Stockport (Tiviot Dale) and all the stations on the MB&M; between Hyde and Macclesfield and between Macclesfield and all stations on the MB&M and Disley (via Middlewood); between Bollington and High Lane, Middlewood and Rose Hill (not Poynton!!). In July 1893, these facilities were extended to between Manchester (Central) and the MB&M stations, and between Oldham and Macclesfield. Apprentices' tickets at half rates were available to Apprentices (in receipt of nominal wages), students and governesses, under 18 years of age.

Workmen's tickets were advertised in November 1892 in the MS&L timetable, but, as far as the MB&M was concerned, were available only between Macclesfield and Bollington; these facilities were available between Macclesfield and Bollington on 7.10 a.m. on the outward journey, and after 5 p.m. (weekdays) and noon (Saturdays) on the return. Between Bollington and Macclesfield, travel was on the 8.43 a.m. train only on the outward journey and the same arrangements, as above, for the return. By 1899, Workmen's ticket facilities had been extended to between Poynton and Bollington, and Bollington and High Lane. Workmen's tickets were available for 6 days – Monday to Saturday inclusive – and for one journey in each direction in 3rd class only.

The November 1891 timetable contained details of fares for passengers and rates for horses and carriages to and from London. Single and return tickets were available for 1st and 3rd class to all MB&M stations, but rates for horses and carriages applied only to Macclesfield (Central) and Bollington because of lack of facilities at the other stations; the facilities at Bollington were no longer available in 1903. By way of illustration, a 3rd class return ticket from London to Macclesfield was 27s. 6d., horses 45s. 9d. each single journey, and carriages 59s. each single journey.

The railways by this time were advertising more extensively their excursion arrangements, and there was increasing evidence of closer co-operation between the MS&L and the NS. Fishing parties were included in the tourist arrangements in November 1891, with tickets (3rd class return only) being issued to fishermen upon production of rod and line at the time of booking, which also had to be produced when tickets were examined. There were excursions from Macclesfield (Central) and Bollington to Buxton (Midland), Chapel (Midland), Knutsford, Plumbley, Lostock Gralam, Northwich, Doncaster, Worksop, Lincoln, Retford, and others; there were excursions from Warrington to Poynton and Macclesfield, from Hyde, Woodley, Romiley and Marple to Macclesfield, and from Romiley to Rudyard. From the MS&L stations there were excursion

Rose Hill Station
c1909

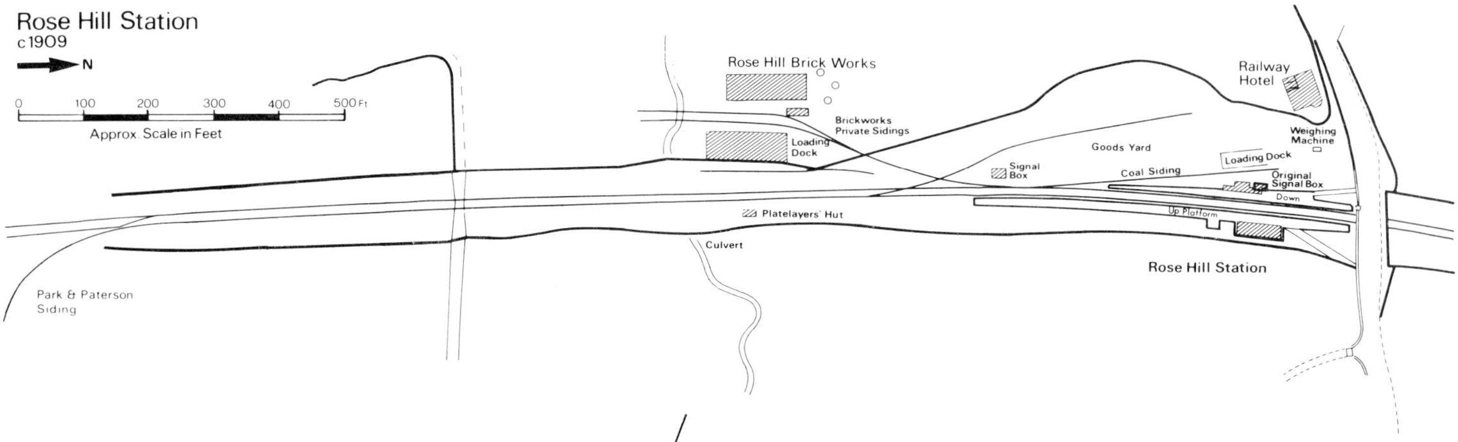

High Lane Station
c 1898

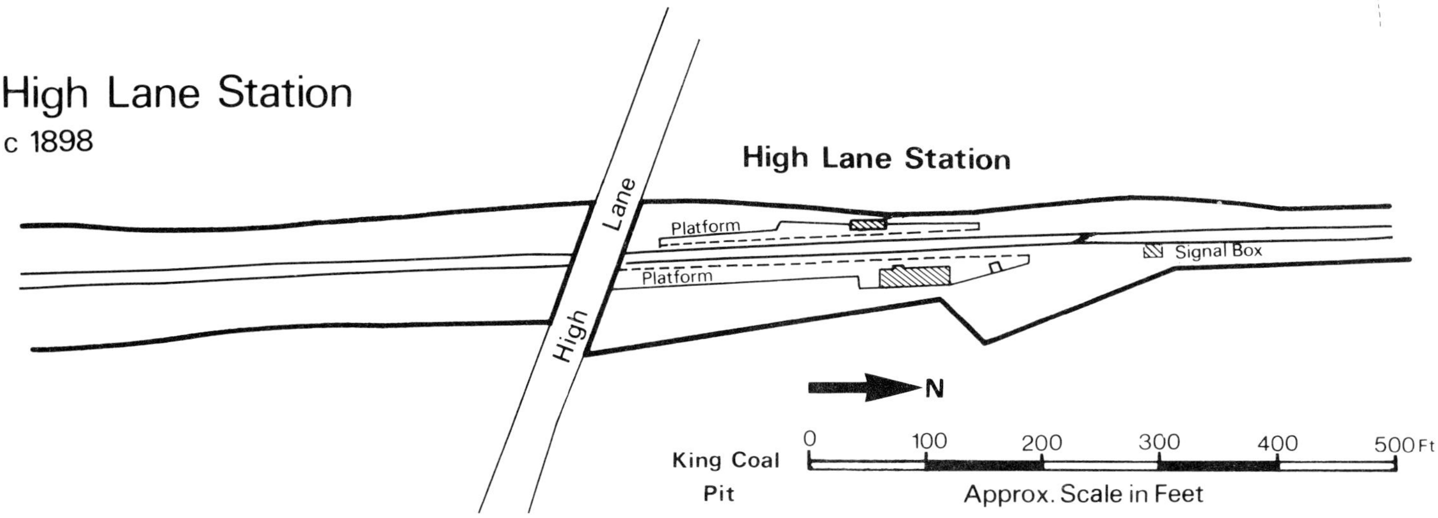

Bollington Station
c 1909

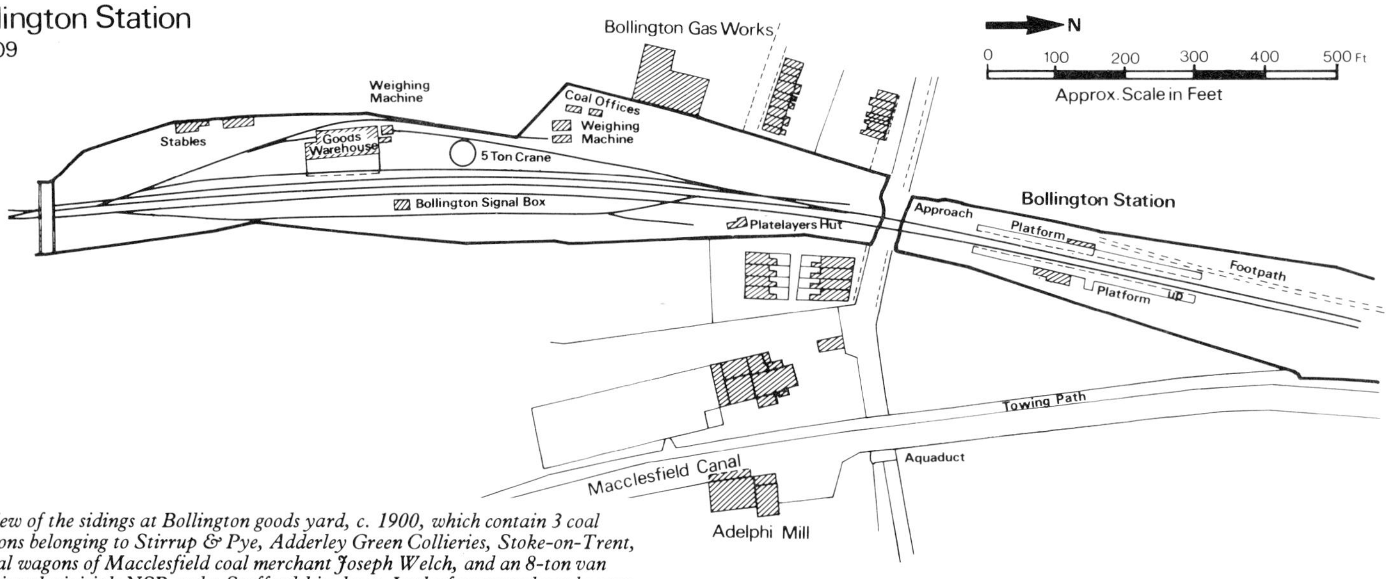

A view of the sidings at Bollington goods yard, c. 1900, which contain 3 coal wagons belonging to Stirrup & Pye, Adderley Green Collieries, Stoke-on-Trent, 2 coal wagons of Macclesfield coal merchant Joseph Welch, and an 8-ton van bearing the initials NSR and a Staffordshire knot. In the foreground can be seen the chimney of the Bollington Gas Works, whilst on the right in the centre of the picture can be seen several wooden coal offices. G. A. Price collection.

rates from London Road, Ashburys, Ashton (Park Parade and Oldham Road), Stalybridge, Guide Bridge and Oldham (Clegg Street and Glodwick Road) to stations on the NS network – Rudyard, North Rode, Clifton, Ashbourne, Derby and Buxton – as well as to Poynton and Macclesfield (Central).

There were excursion arrangements from Macclesfield (Central) via the MB&M, 1st and 3rd class, all over the country, and on a more restricted basis from Bollington; the only MS&L excursion available from Poynton was to the Isle of Man via the CLC. There were none from the other stations on the MB&M. The MB&M route was also used by the MS&L in offering excursion rates to Dovedale and Alton Towers, from places as far afield as Grimsby, Sheffield, Doncaster, Lincoln, Wigan, Chester, Liverpool and Warrington.

The NS "Tourist Arrangements" for 1899 offered excursions to Buxton with day tickets on Mondays, Thursdays and Saturdays, half day tickets on Saturdays, as well as weekend tickets; the 3rd class half day tickets from Macclesfield and Bollington cost 1s. 9d., and 2s. in 1906. The attraction of tourists from the Potteries to Buxton via the MB&M was much reduced because of the opportunities to travel via Ashbourne and the L&NW route to Buxton.

The opening of the "Toy" railway – the Leek and Manifold Valley Light Railway – in 1904, and the connecting rail link from Leek to Waterhouses in 1905, provided the opportunity in 1906 for the NS to provide cheap excursion tickets from Bollington and Macclesfield (Central) to Waterhouses and the Manifold Valley on Mondays, Wednesdays, Saturdays and Sundays in the summer months.

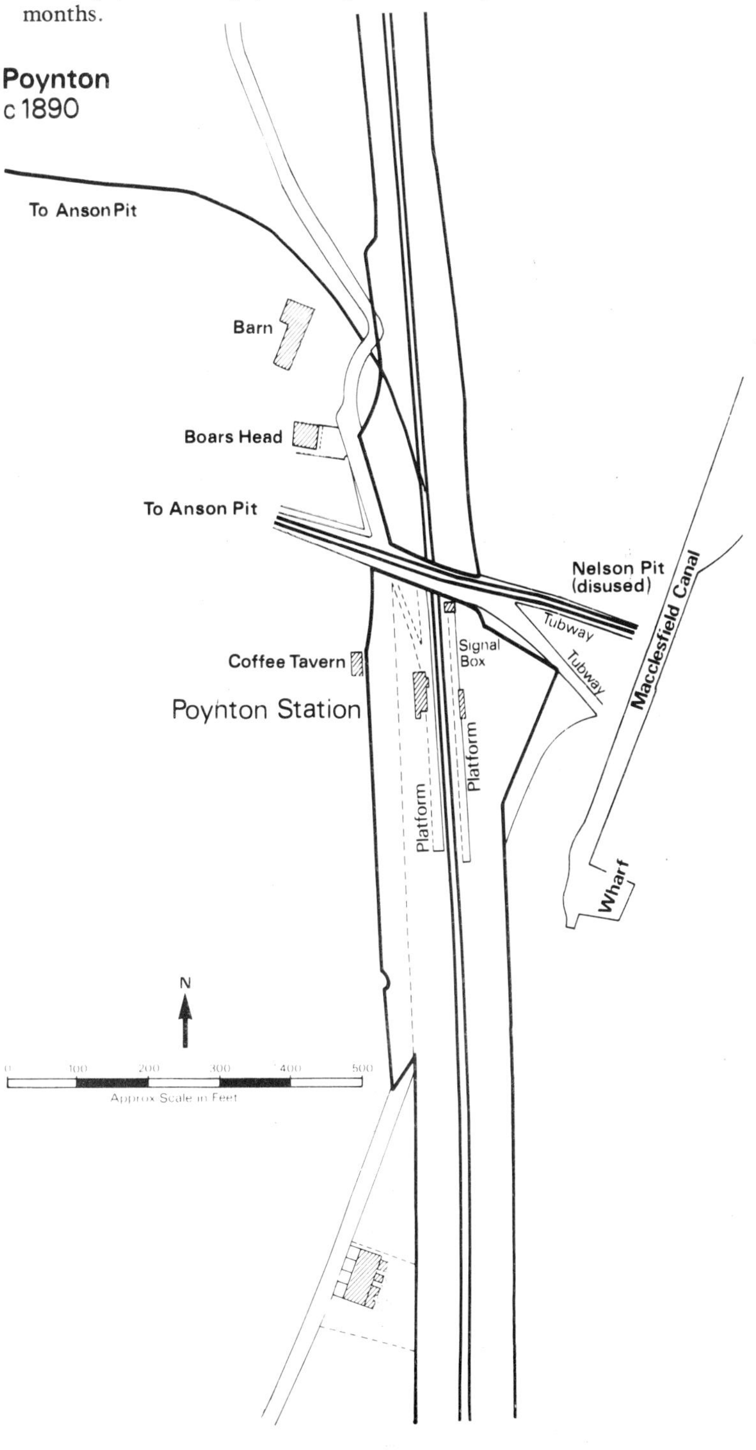

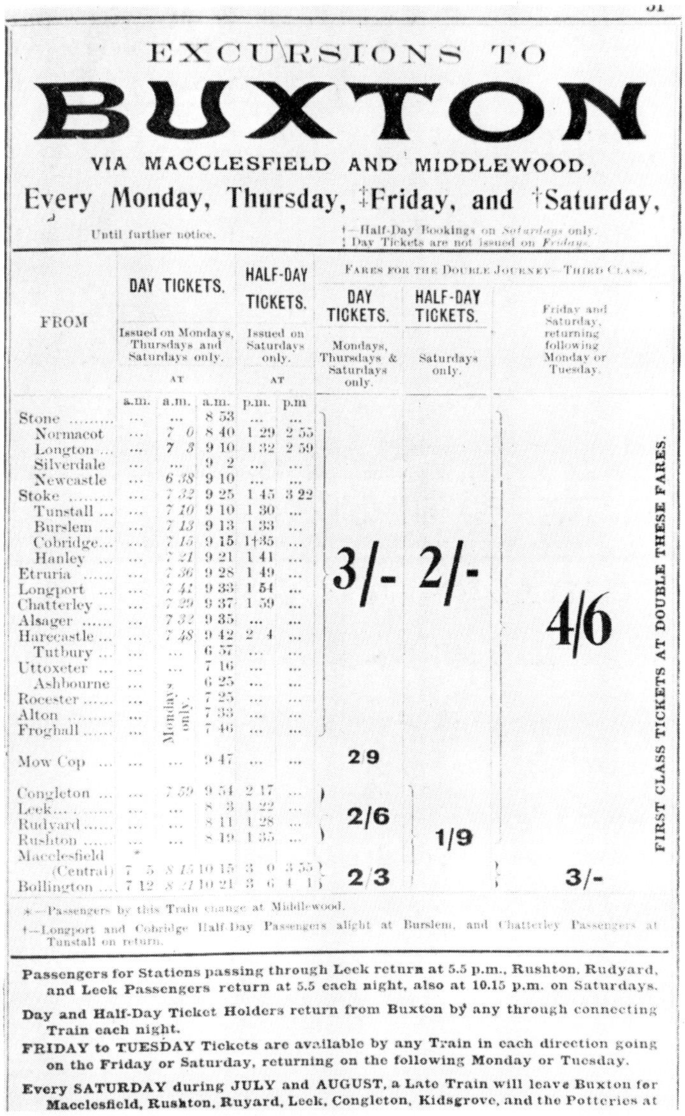

EXCURSIONS TO

BUXTON

VIA MACCLESFIELD AND MIDDLEWOOD,

Every Monday, Thursday, ‡Friday, and †Saturday,

Until further notice.

†—Half-Day Bookings on *Saturdays* only.
‡ Day Tickets are not issued on *Fridays*.

FROM	DAY TICKETS. Issued on Mondays, Thursdays and Saturdays only. AT			HALF-DAY TICKETS. Issued on Saturdays only. AT		Fares for the Double Journey—Third Class. DAY TICKETS. Mondays, Thursdays & Saturdays only.	HALF-DAY TICKETS. Saturdays only.	Friday and Saturday, returning following Monday or Tuesday.
	a.m.	a.m.	a.m.	p.m.	p.m			
Stone	...	...	8 53	...	...			
Normacot	...	7 0	8 40	1 29	2 55			
Longton	...	7 3	9 10	1 32	2 59			
Silverdale	...	...	9 2	...	...			
Newcastle	...	6 38	9 10	...	...			
Stoke	...	7 32	9 25	1 45	3 22			
Tunstall	...	7 10	9 10	1 30	...			
Burslem	...	7 13	9 13	1 33	...			
Cobridge	...	7 15	9 15	1†35	...			
Hanley	...	7 21	9 21	1 41	...			
Etruria	...	7 36	9 28	1 49	...	3/-	2/-	
Longport	...	7 41	9 33	1 54	...			
Chatterley	...	7 29	9 37	1 59	...			
Alsager	...	7 32	9 35	...	...			
Harecastle	...	7 48	9 42	2 4	...			4/6
Tutbury	...	...	6 57	...	...			
Uttoxeter	...	...	7 16	...	...			
Ashbourne	...		6 25	...	...			
Rocester	...	Mondays only.	7 25	...	...			
Alton	...		7 33	...	...			
Froghall	...		7 46	...	...			
Mow Cop	...	...	9 47	...	...	2/9		
Congleton	...	7 59	9 54	2 17	...			
Leek	...	...	8 3	1 22	...	2/6		
Rudyard	...	...	8 11	1 28	...			
Rushton	...	...	8 19	1 35	...		1/9	
Macclesfield (Central)	* 7 5	8 15	10 15	3 0	3 55	2/3		3/-
Bollington	7 12	8 21	10 21	3 6	4 1			

FIRST CLASS TICKETS AT DOUBLE THESE FARES.

*—Passengers by this Train change at Middlewood.

†—Longport and Cobridge Half-Day Passengers alight at Burslem, and Chatterley Passengers at Tunstall on return.

Passengers for Stations passing through Leek return at 5.5 p.m., Rushton, Rudyard, and Leek Passengers return at 5.5 each night, also at 10.15 p.m. on Saturdays.

Day and Half-Day Ticket Holders return from Buxton by any through connecting Train each night.

FRIDAY to TUESDAY Tickets are available by any Train in each direction going on the Friday or Saturday, returning on the following Monday or Tuesday.

Every SATURDAY during JULY and AUGUST, a Late Train will leave Buxton for Macclesfield, Rushton, Ruyard, Leek, Congleton, Kidsgrove, and the Potteries at

This advertisement, designed to boost excursion traffic from the Potteries over the Middlewood curve to Buxton, appeared in the North Staffordshire Railway Tourist Arrangements, Season (July) 1899. Author's collection.

Higher Poynton station in the early 1960's looking north. Note the signal box on the right hand side with a very restricted view of traffic approaching from Middlewood. Author's collection.

The CLC (which was part owned by the GC) in 1905 offered a very interesting range of walking and cycling tours in Lancashire, Derbyshire, Cheshire and North Wales, tickets being available to return by any Ordinary train on the day of issue. One excursion was from Liverpool (Central) to Macclesfield (Central), via the MB&M, with the return rail journey being from Chester (Northgate) to Liverpool Landing Stage; the 3rd class rail fare was 3s. 5d. plus 1s. 6d. for the bike, the excursionist having to cycle the 38 miles between Macclesfield and Chester. The CLC passenger timetable for the same year advertised a service between Liverpool, Southport, Warrington, Stockport and Macclesfield; from Macclesfield there were 10 services daily and 3 on Sundays, whilst from Liverpool there were 8 daily and 3 on Sundays. The connections at Stockport

(Tiviot Dale) and at Romiley were generally not satisfactory – the quickest journey time 1 hour 55 minutes and the longest 3 hours 40 minutes.

The MB&M was used regularly by the Poynton miners for their excursions. In June 1890, 500 miners and their wives and friends, and brass band, went to Southport where they assembled on the

London & North Western, Macclesfield Bollington & Marple, and North Stafford Railways.

NEW EXPRESS ROUTE TO BUXTON

FROM LONDON, BIRMINGHAM, NOTTINGHAM, LICHFIELD, DERBY, BURTON AND THE POTTERIES.

OCTOBER, 1888.—WEEK DAYS ONLY.

	STATIONS.	a.m.	a.m.	a.m.	noon	p.m.	
L. & N. W. Railway	LONDON (Eus.) dep.	...	5 15	7 30	12 0	4 0	...
	OXFORD ... ... „	...	...	...	9 50	2 30	...
	CAMBRIDGE ...... „	...	...	...	7 50	1 55	...
	N'HAMPTON (C.S.) „	...	6 39	9 10	12 50	4 34	...
	RUGBY ... „	...	7 12	9 41	1 53	5 52	...
	LEICESTER ... ... „	...	6 45	8 20	11 35	4 30	...
	TAMWORTH ... „	...	7 51	10 18	1 57	6 1	...
	LICHFIELD ... ... „	...	8 4	10 31	2 36	6 33	...
	BIRMINGHAM (N. S.) „	6 0	7 30	9 30	12g15	4 50	...
	W'HAMPTON (H. Level) „	6 40	7 59	10 16	12g20	5 20	...
N.S.R.	Stafford ... dep.	7 25	9 5	10 58	12 53	5 50	...
	Stone ... ... „	7 43	9 25	11 14	2 11	6 10	...
G. N. Ry.	PETERBORO' dep.	12 24	...	6 49	10 52	2 7	...
	Boston ... ... „	...	...	7 48	9 15	1 5	...
	LINCOLN ... „	...	...	7 30	10 23	1 50	...
	Newark ... ... „	12 0	...	9 3	9 47	3 3	...
	NOTTINGHAM ... „	5 50	...	9 53	12 35	3 30	...
N. S. Railway	DERBY ... ... „	6c38	8 0	11 0	2 b 0	4 25	...
	BURTON ... „	...	8 0	11 0	2 b 0	4 20	...
	Uttoxeter ... ... „	7 16	9 5	12 20	2b40	5 30	...
	Ashbourne ... „	6 45	8 5	11 0	2 b 5	5 20	...
	Alton ... ... „	7 34	9 25	12 38	...	5 50	...
	Leek ... „	8 1	9 54	1 6	2b20	6 17	...
	Rudyard ... ... „	8 6	10 0	1 11	...	6 22	...
	Longton ... „	7 45	9 29	11 15	3 4	6 45	...
	Newcastle ... ... „	7 52	9 36	11 1	3 0	7 6	...
	STOKE ... dep.	8 5	9 50	11 28	3 19	7 17	...
	Hanley ... ... „	7 44	9 44	11b14	2b44	7 b 4	...
	Etruria ... „	8 10	9 53	11b19	2b49	7 b 9	...
	Harecastle (Kidsgrove) „	8 23	10 6	11 13	1 55	5 44	...
	Congleton ... „	8 36	10 19	11 26	2 8	5 55	...
	Macclesfield ... ... „	9 e 0	10e45	1d43	3e55	7d45	...
M.B.&M.	Bollington ... dep	9 5	10 52	...	4 2	...	...
	Middlewood ... ... „	9 47	...	...	...	8a50	...
L. & N. W.	Disley ... arr.	9 52	l	2a47	l	8a55	...
	New Mills ... ... „	9 56	l	2a51	l	8a59	...
	Whaley Bridge ... „	10 4	l	2a59	l	9 a 7	...
	Chapel-en-le-frith „	10 13	l	3 a 8	l	9a16	...
	BUXTON ... „	10 27	11 25	3a22	4 35	9a30	...

	STATIONS.	a.m.	a.m.	a.m.	p.m.	p.m.	p.m.
L. & N. W.	BUXTON dep.	7a 0	9 a 0	11 45	1 15	5 0	...
	Chapel-en-le-frith „	7a13	9a10	m	1 29	m	...
	Whaley Bridge ... „	7a21	8a51	m	1 37	m	...
	New Mills ... „	7a28	9a20	m	1 45	m	...
	Disley ... ... „	7a32	9 a 3	m	1 50	m	...
	Middlewood ... „	7a36	...	...	3 34	...	...
M.B.&M.	Bollington ... arr.	...	...	12 17	3 45	5 32	...
N. S. Railway	Macclesfield ... arr.	8d44	10d14	12e23	3e52	5e38	...
	Congleton ... „	9 0	10 31	...	4 28	6 18	...
	Harecastle (Kidsgrove) ... „	9j20	10 43	...	4 42	6j37	...
	Etruria ... ... „	9j49	11b26	1b16	5 3	6b56	...
	Hanley ... „	9j44	11b30	1b20	5 15	7 b 0	...
	STOKE ... ... „	9 17	10 54	1 5	5 8	6 37	...
	Newcastle ... arr.	9 26	11 6	1 35	5 17	6 46	...
	Longton ... ... „	9 35	11 30	1 30	5 30	7 0	...
	Rudyard ... „	...	10 49	1f18	...	6 39	...
	Leek ... ... „	...	10 54	1f24	6 b 5	6 45	...
	Alton ... „	...	11 19	1f51	...	7 13	...
	Ashbourne ... ... „	...	12 52	3h20	...	7 50	...
	Uttoxeter ... „	...	11 36	2k10	...	7 30	...
	BURTON ... ... „	...	12 53	3n20	...	8 21	...
	DERBY ... „	...	12 57	3n20	...	8 30	...
G. N. Ry.	NOTTINGHAM ... „	...	2 1	4 44	...	9 38	...
	Newark ... „	...	2 42	5 32	...	11 14	...
	LINCOLN ... ... „	...	3 53	6 28	...	...	...
	Boston ... „	...	4 41	7 13	...	3 28	...
	PETERBORO' „	...	3 38	6 12	...	12 22	...
N.S.R.	Stone ... arr.	9 42	11 9	2p34	5 30	6 55	...
	Stafford ... ... „	9 59	11 25	1 44	5 48	7 8	...
L. & N. W. Railway	W'HAMPTON (H. Level) arr.	10 29	11 56	2 15	6 25	7 38	...
	BIRMINGHAM (N.S.) „	10 55	12 25	2 40	7 0	8 10	...
	LICHFIELD ... „	11 35	11 59	2 5	7 46	7 46	...
	TAMWORTH ... ... „	12 16	12 16	2 17	8 0	8 0	...
	LEICESTER ... „	11 40	1 55	3 47	8 42	9 40	...
	RUGBY ... ... „	10 45	12 48	2 25	8 7	7 55	...
	N'HAMPTON (C. S.) „	11 15	1 18	3 21	8 38	8 38	...
	CAMBRIDGE ... „	3 44	3 44	6 13	...	...	...
	OXFORD ... „	2 55	...	5 26	10 21	...	...
	LONDON (Eus.) ... „	12 40	2 55	4 20	10 15	9 45	...

a—*Via* Stockport, L. & N. W. b—*Via* Stoke. c—From the G. N. Station. d—Hibel Road Station. e—Central Station. f—Wednesdays and Saturdays only. On other days Passengers for Leek travel *via* Stoke and arrive at 2 5. g—*Via* Rugeley. h—Wednesdays and Saturdays *via* the Churnet Line, and on other days *via* Stoke and Uttoxeter. j—Passengers change at Congleton. k—Wednesdays and Saturdays *via* the Churnet Line and on other days *via* Stoke, reaching Uttoxeter at 2 43. l—Calls to set down Passengers only. m—Calls to pick up Passengers only for Macclesfield and beyond. n—Wednesdays and Saturdays *via* the Churnet Line and on other days *via* Stoke. p—On Saturdays Passengers can arrive at Stone at 1 29 p.m.

This advertisement appeared in the passenger timetable books of the North Staffordshire Railway for 1888, and was similar to those appearing in the 1887 and 1886 passenger timetable books. Author's collection.

MS&L 2-4-0, Class 8, 68, in February 1886 was shedded at Gorton and diagrammed for passenger working to and from Macclesfield. Built in 1871, it was scrapped in 1903. W. A. Brown collection.

sands with the Ashton District Miners' Association, with which they were associated; in June 1901, a similar excursion was run to the Lancashire and Cheshire Miners' Demonstration, also at Southport.

Between 1887 and 1905, there was some working of MS&L services on the summer Saturdays over the NS network via the MB&M; there was a Manchester (London Road) to Alton train in 1891, 1893, 1896, 1897 and 1898, and to Ashbourne in 1890 and 1894 (when an MS&L engine was derailed); from July to September 1892, the L&NW worked forward MS&L carriages from Macclesfield to both Alton and Trentham. In the summers of 1902 and 1903, there were GC excursions from Manchester on Saturdays to Leek, Oakamoor, Alton, Ashbourne and Uttoxeter, and on Sundays to Rudyard and Leek. The summers of 1893 and 1896 also saw passenger excursions on Saturdays from Macclesfield to Oldham.

MS&L 0-6-0, Class 18, 19 was a Gorton goods engine diagrammed in February 1886 between Ardwick, Macclesfield, Godley and Manchester. W. A. Brown collection.

Turning now to goods and freight working, the opening of the Middlewood curve led to the introduction of a goods service between Macclesfield and Buxton on 1 August 1885. In March 1887, the pattern of working was for an NS locomotive from Macclesfield to work wagons to Middlewood leaving them in the "exchange" sidings, and to return to Macclesfield with the wagons that had been left by 2 L&NW trains, the 6.30 a.m. Whaley Bridge to Edgeley Junction mineral train, and the 2.05 p.m. Buxton to Longsight goods; wagons left at the "exchange" sidings were taken forward on the 7 a.m. Longsight to Buxton goods. Working the exchange on a 1 train each way basis continued until 1946, though through working between Buxton and Macclesfield did not start until the mid-1920s.

The impact of the curve on the sales from Poynton Collieries was considerable, as it was able to sell its output on the L&NW network as the following table shows:

	1884 (Tons)	*1889 (Tons)*	*1896 (Tons)*
New Mills	423	3,060	1,101
Whaley Bridge	162	2,779	9,668
Buxton	24	1,292	1,735
	609	7,131	12,504

In 1897, coal traffic from Poynton Collieries along the MB&M to stations on the MS&L network totalled 28,082 tons (mainly to Reddish and Woodley, though for the first time more coal went to Bollington by rail than by canal); including the traffic over the curve, 18% of the Collieries' output in 1897 went via the MB&M. In that year 3,493 tons went to Bollington and 1,609 tons to Rose Hill from the Collieries via MB&M; competition from the Macclesfield canal was reduced in 1892 when the MS&L ceased to be carriers on the canal.

Milk traffic from Macclesfield, Bollington and Poynton was allowed on a limited number of trains daily to a certain number of nearby stations, including Middlewood, High Lane, Rose Hill, Hyde, Oldham, Stalybridge and Ardwick; the rate charged in 1891 was for cans not exceeding 18 gallons 1s. 0d., and for cans over 18, and not exceeding 21 gallons, 1s. 6d.

The next information that exists on goods working on the MB&M is derived from the GC and NS working timetables of October and November 1899. From Macclesfield there were 2 daily express GC goods trains to Godley (1 on Mondays), and 2 ordinary goods trains; there were 2 express goods daily for the CLC, except Mondays, 1 to Huskisson docks at Liverpool and 1 to Heaton Mersey exchange sidings; on Sundays there was a GC goods and express goods to Godley, and a CLC goods to both Huskisson and Heaton Mersey. Into Macclesfield there was daily a GC express goods and ordinary goods from Godley, a daily (Saturdays excepted) express CLC goods from Huskisson, a daily (Mondays excepted) express CLC goods from Heaton Mersey, and an ordinary CLC goods on Saturdays from Heaton Mersey. This frequency of service represents a considerable strengthening compared to the levels in the late 1870s; the Huskisson service brought cotton from the Liverpool docks to the mills at Rose Hill, Bollington and Macclesfield.

At that time the NS had its own workings over the MB&M. There was a daily Cliffe Vale to Ardwick and a daily Stoke to Ardwick goods service, a Saturdays only Stoke to Godley through goods, and a Stoke to Godley ordinary goods (Saturdays and Mondays excepted). The return workings consisted of 2 daily ordinary goods from Ardwick to Stoke, 1 Ardwick to Longton on Sundays, a daily Godley to Stoke ordinary goods (Mondays excepted), and a through goods from Godley to Longton. In addition, exchange traffic at Macclesfield from the NS came from Stoke, Burton, Adderley Green, Rocester, and Uttoxeter, and there were return workings to

Former MS&L 0-6-0, Class 18, renumbered as 5B in GC days, and converted to a saddle tank in 1904, was another Gorton goods engine of 1886 on the Macclesfield run. W. A. Brown collection.

the same destinations. In September 1900, the NS ceased to work over the GC line to Ardwick and Godley, and this was replaced by the NS with an extra daily goods train each way between Sideway, Stoke, and Macclesfield (Mondays excepted), and an extra fish train (Wednesdays to Saturdays) from Macclesfield. The GC, for its part, in May 1901 converted the 7.20 p.m. Macclesfield to Godley express goods to a Macclesfield to Ardwick express goods and a service to Ardwick remained until about 1961.

The period from 1885 to 1907, as far as information is available, was one of improved fortunes for the MC. In the 3 years to June 1888, a net loss of only £21 was sustained – a vast improvement on previous years; it would appear that no losses were sustained until 1900. The following table shows the growth in receipts between 1885 and 1900:

Year	*Passenger* £	*Goods* £	*Minerals* £	*Total* £
1885	6,280	10,422		16,702
1889	8,401	10,016	3,745	22,162
1895	9,339	15,503	3,486	28,328
1900	9,928	17,969	4,871	32,768

During the period under review, passenger revenue increased by more than half, whilst revenue from goods and minerals traffic more than doubled.

This period of profitability was to prove relatively shortlived as major engineering costs were soon to be faced.

The pride of the locomotive driver and fireman is seen in this photograph taken in July 1904 at exchange sidings, Macclesfield, of NS 0-6-2T, L Class, 124. Thomas Baskville and Nat Eccles pose with a spotless locomotive. Manifold collection.

7 The Great Central and North Staffordshire Railway Committee - 1907 to 1930

During the period from 1907 to 1930, the MB&M was managed by the GC/NS, and after 1930 until nationalisation it was managed by the London and North Eastern Railway (LNE) and London, Midland and Scottish Railway (LMS) in their Group Committee No. 1. The 23 years of the GC/NS were difficult ones for the railways generally - there was the 1st World War and the depression of the 1920's, prolonged industrial action in 1911, 1919 and 1921, the General Strike of 1926, and growing competition of road transport and road haulage. The "Grouping" of the many railway companies in 1923 was intended to lead to streamlining and rationalisation of services; despite "Grouping", the GC/NS did not lose its identity immediately as an organisation separately managed, but lasted until 1930.

1910 saw approval given for the reconstruction of the railway bridge at Buxton Road, Macclesfield, at a cost of £858; the original construction was for a much lighter working load. Mining subsidence at Poynton led to £498 being spent on raising an overbridge in 1910, and a landslip in the same year cost a further £235. In 1911, a Bill was promoted in Parliament, the Macclesfield and District Railless Traction and Electricity Supply Bill, which contained powers to work trolley vehicles along certain railless routes for passengers, goods and animals; these routes included the Macclesfield to Bollington route and clearly represented a threat to the MB&M. The Bill was resisted and eventually dropped later in the year.

The MB&M was caught up in the national railway strike between 17 and 19 August 1911, although there had been disruption for a few days before; in Macclesfield, Hibel Road was affected, though Central station traffic was not interfered with. The strike call came to Macclesfield from the Amalgamated Society of Railway Servants at 9 p.m. on Thursday 17 August and night staff immediately left work; 200-300 men came out, both union and non-union workers, covering all grades - drivers, stokers, cleaners, porters, signalmen, carters - though it was agreed that the railway clerks could stay at work performing their own duties only. On 18 August, only 1 train each way went on the MB&M, and none on the Saturday; the pointsman worked the signal box (Maclesfield Junction) at Brunswick Hill initially, but was later "influenced by the persuasion of pickets"! Although the strike was called off on 19 August, Bollington, which at that time had 15 railway workers affected, did not see resumption of full service for a further 3 days; the farmers and milk producers in the area had to convey their produce by road to Hazel Grove.

In the Autumn of 1911, 2 water columns were erected at Poynton, for £309, to facilitate working and to economise in expenses; the water was to come from the nearby Macclesfield canal which was owned by the GC.

1911 and 1912 was a period of industrial unrest. "Memorials" had been received from every branch of the GC/NS's employees for an advance in wages and a reduction in hours, but the question was left in the hands of the NS to deal with, since these employees were included in the NS conciliation schemes. On 29 February 1912, a national coal strike started, with 700 miners out at Anson, Lawrance and Park Pits. Many of the passenger services on the MB&M were stopped for a month, and GC/NS employees were sworn in as special constables to protect railway and other property; work at the pits resumed on 13 April, but not before the Poynton Branch of the Miners' Association had paid out £1,829 in strike pay.

In 1913, a 5-ton hand-powered wharf crane was purchased for Bollington at a cost of £142. In 1914, J. Crosbie-Dawson, the Engineer to the MB&M as well as to the NS, died, and was replaced by F. A. L. Barnwell, then Engineer to the NS and later to become its last General Manager. It was reported to the Board Meeting on 22 October 1914 that, under the Regulation of the Forces Act 1871, the Government had taken control of the railways with effect from 4 August 1914, and an agreed basis for calculating compensation, provided for in the Act, had been received from the Railway Executive Committee. At the same meeting it was agreed to discontinue insurance of buildings with the Atlas Assurance - which were then worth £11,220 - and to make a provision through its own insurance reserve fund at a 25th of the value. In 1914 and 1915, bridges were repaired at Bollington for £350, Rose Hill for £225, and Bollington again for £239; these engineering costs were to prove to be the forerunner of much worse to come.

In October 1916, Barnwell reported that extensive repairs were needed to the Bollington Goods Yard, because the ordinary metalling was cutting up badly due to heavy motor traffic; £543 was approved. He also advocated spending money on Macclesfield Goods Yard, because of wear, and this was agreed to at £575. In November 1917, Barnwell pointed out the need for at least one mile of track to be re-laid each year; since the war started only 629 yards had been re-laid, and he warned that speed curtailments might be necessary. More serious was his report in February 1918, on the general condition of the viaduct over the River Bollin at Macclesfield; one section was one-third under strength, and because of the weight of modern traffic, 7 spans were under strength. Barnwell concluded that the cost of reconstruction would amount to £12,500 and that until the Government gave approval for the purchase of steel (which was in short supply because of the war) traffic over the viaduct would need to be one train at a time. This approval was only secured early in 1919, after the war had ended, and a tender for £15,000 from Eastwood Swingler & Co., of Derby, was accepted (the bulk of it being for steel work at £29 per ton); the NS and the GC were each to pay half.

The viaduct through the Macclesfield Gas Works and straddling the River Bollin needed regular and costly maintenance. A GC crane is here being used to lower a beam being put into place, with the Gas Works towers dominating the skyline. Manifold collection.

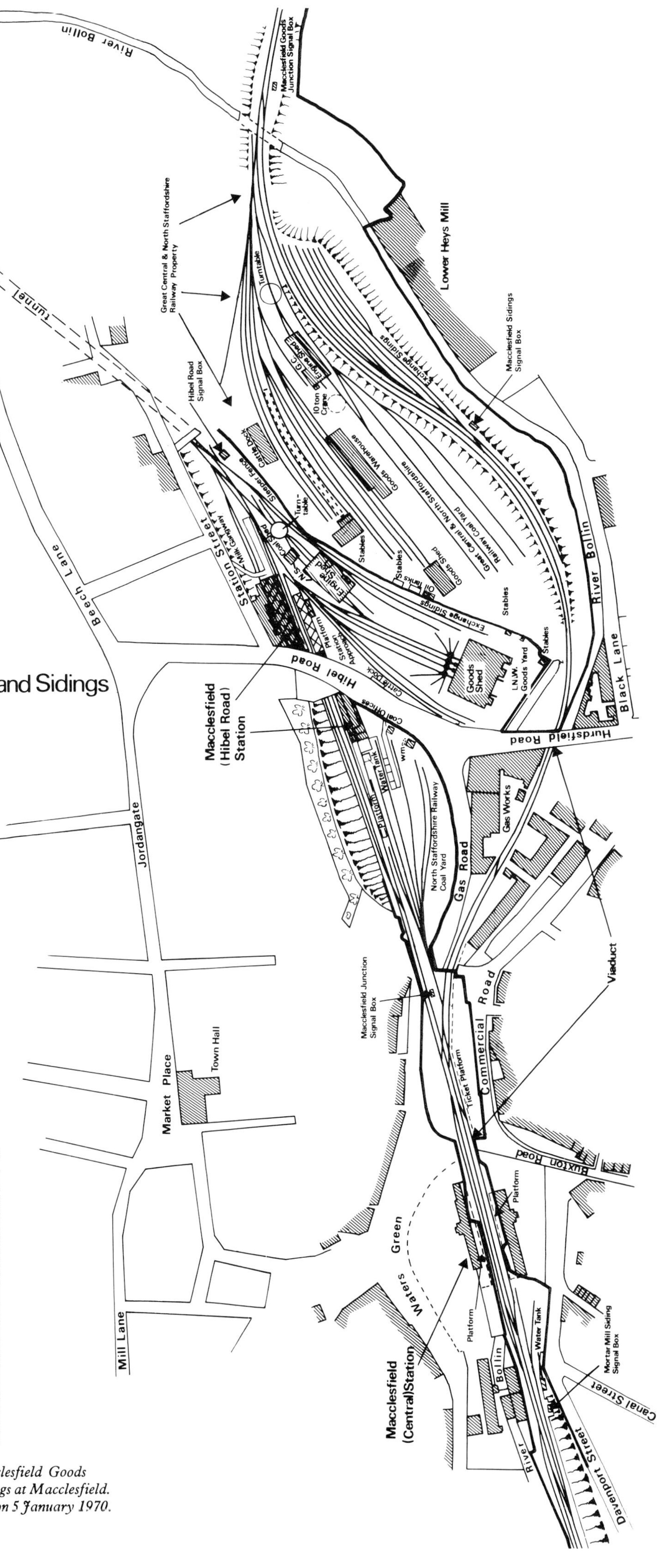

Macclesfield Stations, Goods Yards and Sidings c 1912

N

0 100 200 300 400 500 Ft

Approx. Scale in Feet

One of the tallest signal boxes of Knotty design was the Macclesfield Goods Junction box, located a few yards north of the exchange sidings at Macclesfield. This photograph was taken a few days before the line closed on 5 January 1970. M. Welch.

The reconstruction of the viaduct was a major engineering exercise which cut off Central station from the MB&M line; work was carried out on Sundays, starting on 7 September 1919, and, to deal with local passenger traffic, the existing platform of the old station (used as a temporary station between 1869 and 1873) was used on various Sundays until 23 November. The effect on goods traffic on these Sundays was that no through vehicles or traffic for exchange to or from the NS line, via the MB&M, could be transferred at Macclesfield. For the reconstruction work, a special train left Stoke for Macclesfield at midnight with NS Engineer's men and crane, whilst a second train (from Stoke) conveyed the L&NW steam crane and men from Crewe to Macclesfield; a GC traffic inspector controlled passenger traffic into the old station – all in all, a team effort. The NS Engineer had possession of the line on each occasion from 2 a.m. Sunday until 6 a.m. Monday. The final cost amounted to £17,450, £2,450 above the amount originally authorised.

Work on repairing the viaduct had been delayed in September and October, because of a strike arising from a national conflict between the railway companies and its employees. The cause of the strike was the level of wages after the war, against the background of the increased cost of living during and immediately after the war years. Railwaymen were offered an increase of 100% on the pre-war wage levels; railwaymen were then getting a war-time bonus of 33s. above pre-war wages and this was planned to continue until the end of 1919. The problem facing the railwaymen was that, in many cases before the war, wages were so low that doubling the pre-war wages would not give as good a result as the 33s. extra. The strike lasted from Friday night, 26 September, to Monday 6 October and spoiled the Macclesfield Wakes holiday; in Macclesfield, between 500 and 600 men of all grades were involved, the NUR and ASLE&F obeyed the call to strike, whilst the clerks, inspectors, and station masters, who were members of the Railway Clerks Association, were advised to remain neutral. Milk traffic was particularly affected, though some reached its destination by lorry, and there was considerable disruption of mail. The Miners' strike from 15 October to 12 November 1920 and another from 1 April to 1 July 1921 caused considerable disruption on the MB&M, as did the General Strike of May 1926.

Other engineering work carried out around that time was for 2 fog signalling machines at Marple Wharf Junction (the cost of £473 was shared with the Great Central and Midland Joint Railway Committee), the construction of a siding in 1919 at Rose Hill for Park and Paterson (Manchester) Limited, who had established a non-ferrous metal foundry on the site of a disused brickworks, the re-building of the bridge at Middlewood in 1922 for £3,652, the repairing of Bollington goods yard in 1922 for £2,380, whilst further land slippage north of Rose Hill cost £1,193 to repair through improved drainage. In 1921 Barnwell resigned as Engineer, to be replaced by C. G. Rose, the Engineer to the NS. In October 1921 he brought forward a relaying programme for 1922, costing £14,000; he pointed out the arrears of maintenance and said that there were still 3 miles of the original track laid in 1869 which were in a dangerous condition. This relaying programme was approved by the General Managers of the GC and of the NS.

The "Grouping" of the national railways took place in 1923, under provisions laid down under the Railway Act 1921. The LMS was formed on 1 January, but it was not until 1 July 1923 that it absorbed the NS. Likewise the LNE was formed on 1 January 1923, one of its constituent companies being the GC. There were special arrangements for the various "joint" companies, of which the MB&M was one, which were to become the joint property of the LNE and LMS. New Board members were appointed in March, 1923, Butler-Henderson, Gair, Noble and Trotter for the LNE, and Wedgwood, Dorrington, Behrens and Stockton for the LMS. Their attention was drawn in February 1925 to the deteriorating financial position; the loss for the year to December 1922 had been £7,360, for 1923 £7,748, and for 1924 £17,552. By the time the General Managers of the LNE and LMS reported in October 1926, a further loss of £16,597 had been sustained for 1925. The terms of reference were three-fold; firstly the abnormal expenditure on permanent way maintenance, secondly the high traffic expenses, and thirdly the falling off of "through" traffic carried over the line.

The comments on permanent way maintenance were that costs had been reduced by £520, following the reduction in the number in the gangs from 31 to 27; the question of converting the double line between Rose Hill and Bollington into a single line, in order to reduce maintenance costs further, was to be kept under review. The high traffic expenses were to be reduced by a combination of measures; firstly, the linking up of Station Masters' and Goods Agents' positions, whilst the closing of signal boxes would ultimately yield £1,800; secondly, the rates charged by the LNE and the LMS were reduced, saving a further £1,085; thirdly, the reduction in train mileage was to be kept under continual review. This part of the report provides valuable information on traffic on the MB&M;

Station staff at Middlewood station, c. 1919, in front of the waiting room on the upside. In the centre is Jack Walker, Porter Signalman. Behind can be seen on the left a poster advertising Great Central Railway Season's Excursions to Southport and Liverpool and other places, and on the right the North Staffordshire Railway poster advertising 200 acres of water at Rudyard Lake. J. M. Ryan collection.

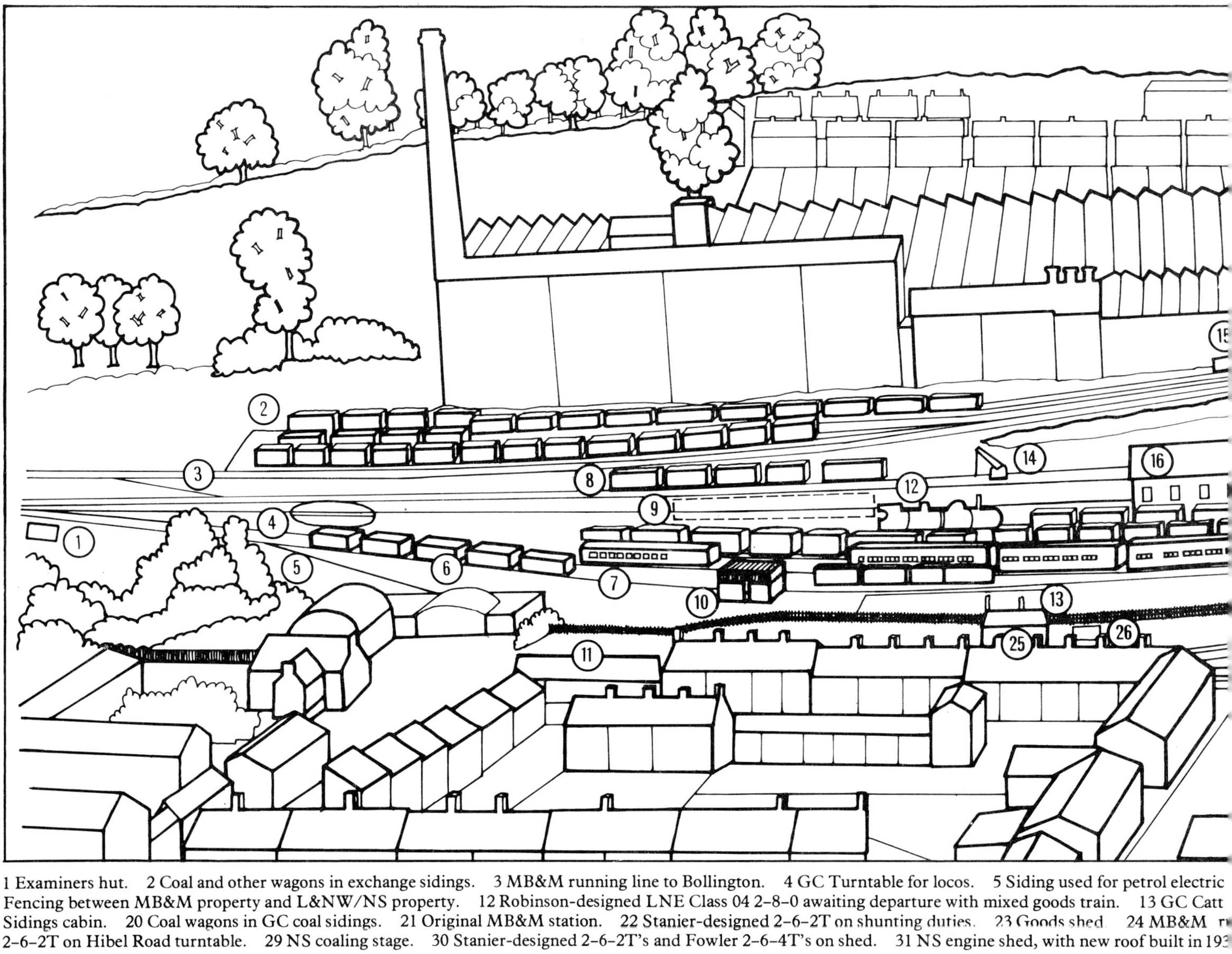

1 Examiners hut. 2 Coal and other wagons in exchange sidings. 3 MB&M running line to Bollington. 4 GC Turntable for locos. 5 Siding used for petrol electric
Fencing between MB&M property and L&NW/NS property. 12 Robinson-designed LNE Class 04 2–8–0 awaiting departure with mixed goods train. 13 GC Catt
Sidings cabin. 20 Coal wagons in GC coal sidings. 21 Original MB&M station. 22 Stanier-designed 2–6–2T on shunting duties. 23 Goods shed. 24 MB&M r
2–6–2T on Hibel Road turntable. 29 NS coaling stage. 30 Stanier-designed 2–6–2T's and Fowler 2–6–4T's on shed. 31 NS engine shed, with new roof built in 193

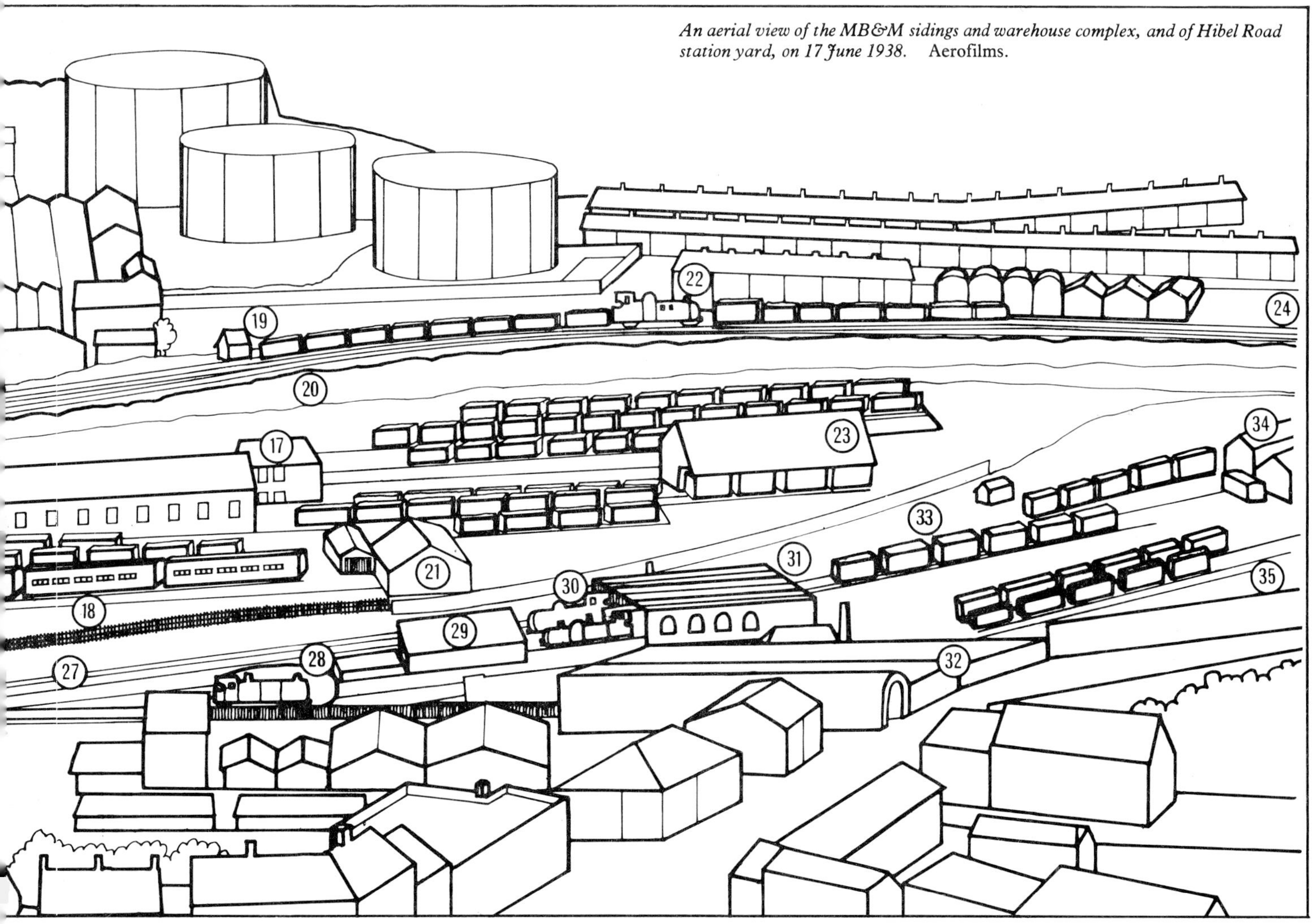

An aerial view of the MB&M sidings and warehouse complex, and of Hibel Road station yard, on 17 June 1938. Aerofilms.

ılcar. 6 Coal wagon in GC sidings. 7 Sentinel steam railcar. 8 Coal wagon in GC coal sidings. 9 Site of GC loco shed. 10 GC Water Tank. 11 Boundary
ock. 14 GC Crane. 15 Examiners hut. 16 Original MB&M Goods Warehouse. 17 Goods Offices. 18 Coach stable sidings with GC carriages. 19 Exchange
ning line to Central station. 25 L&NW Water Tank at Tunnel End. 26 Hibel Road signal box. 27 L&NW running line to Prestbury. 28 Stanier-designed
32 Hibel Road station. 33 L&NW and NS goods exchange sidings. 34 L&NW Goods shed. 35 Cattle dock.

passengers carried in 1924 showed an increase of 26% over 1913, and those carried during 1925 showed an increase of 5% over 1924; season ticket holders increased by 60% compared with pre-war. The General Managers were not satisfied that the introduction of passenger railcar services would improve the financial position.

The position of goods traffic was of concern; the tonnage carried in 1924 and in 1925 showed a decrease of 18% and 25% respectively, compared with pre-war. The cause of loss was not due to any decrease in traffic dealt with at the MB&M stations, but to a decrease in the through traffic; in the case of coal, coke, and patent fuel traffic, the falling off was due to terminated contracts, and in the case of goods and mineral traffic, to the prevailing depression in the iron and steel industry. A reduction in goods train mileage had been achieved and would be kept under review.

High Lane signal box will have been dispensed with at this time. In February 1927, it was agreed to dispense with the Exchange Sidings signal box at Macclesfield and to concentrate working on the Goods Junction signal box; savings from this scheme amounted to £506, mainly through employing 3 less signalmen. In June 1927, the Board established Permanent Way and Bridge Renewal Funds in order to spread the costs equally over many years. In October 1927, contracts were awarded for repainting the stations and bridges at a cost of £730, and the viaduct over the Bollin needed repainting only 4 years after it was last repainted because of extensive corrosion caused by the Gas Works. In October 1929, further construction work was needed on the Bollin Viaduct, and the contract was awarded, for £6,296, to the Horsley Bridge and Engineering Co. Ltd. Despite all the measures to cut costs, losses continued and totalled £53,662 for the 4 years to December 1929.

Various developments were considered during the 1907–1930 period but were not proceeded with. These included extra siding accommodation for 20 wagons at Middlewood in 1925, and a scheme in 1929 at Middlewood for the singling of the curve, the taking out of the flyover, and the putting in of refuge sidings for 35 wagons; a warehouse scheme in 1929 for Star Oil, close to the original MB&M station, was turned down.

There were interesting passenger traffic developments in the period from 1907 to 1929. In April 1910 there were 7 passenger trains daily each way between Central and London Road and 4 on Sundays. To London Road there were 3 via Guide Bridge and 4 via Reddish daily; from London Road there were 6 via Reddish and 1 via Guide Bridge. In addition there was a Saturday afternoon service each way to Hyde Central, and to Woodley, and an extra service to Woodley daily. There was also a morning training each way between Macclesfield and Oldham. In 1921, there were 8 through trains daily each way (5 via Hyde) and an extra 2 services on Saturdays.

Services between Macclesfield and Bollington were of particular interest. In July 1910, the first passenger service was the 5.40 a.m. from Macclesfield, arriving Bollington 5.46 a.m.; the return working was 6.15 a.m. from Bollington, arriving Macclesfield 6.21 a.m. This early service, for mill workers in the main, continued until 1921, though the extension of this service in May 1919 to Poynton was not continued in 1920. By this time the railways were losing passengers to the roads; in Marple, the bus operators soon captured much of the Stockport traffic. Indeed, as early as 1908, Mr. F. J. Clayton of Offerton had been licensed to provide a service between Marple and Stockport; in March 1921, the Marple Urban District Council approved an application from the British Automobile Traction Co. Ltd. of Macclesfield for 23 motor bus and charabanc licenses, and 26 licences for drivers and conductors in the Marple area. Various applications were considered in later years. The GC/NS provided no direct services between Rose Hill and Stockport (Tiviot Dale) and made no attempt to meet the bus competition for this particular traffic. At the Macclesfield end of the line, a petrol electric railcar was introduced on 15 August 1921 between Macclesfield and Bollington primarily; this railcar was built by Westinghouse in 1912 for the GC, and, after service in the Home counties and on the "shuttle" between Glossop and Dinting, it was transferred to Macclesfield in 1921 where it remained until it was withdrawn from service in August 1935. The service was introduced to "combat automobile competition" and, on Fridays and Saturdays, special cheap fares were available at a cost of 6d. return; it was described in the *Macclesfield Courier and Herald* as being "built after the American fashion". In 1921 there were 14 services each way daily by the "Bollington Bug", as it was known; in 1928 there were 13 services each way daily. In 1925, the petrol electric worked a late night service from Macclesfield to Poynton and back, leaving Macclesfield at 10.55 p.m. and arriving at Poynton 11.09 p.m., returning from Poynton at 11.15 p.m.; this particular service enabled Poyntonians to have a late night out in Macclesfield. In 1928, there was also a lunchtime service on Saturdays to Poynton, and a Mondays to Fridays early evening working for the Bug to Romiley, and a corresponding working to Woodley on Saturday evenings.

The Bug, which was stabled in a siding close to the Hibel Road tunnel, had a 90 h.p. engine and was filled up with petrol (18 gallons each time) twice a day; it was serviced at the Dukinfield Wagon Works of the LNE and came under the responsibility of the LNE Electric Department at Guide Gridge. The Bug did not carry any

Taking water and well-coaled is former MS&L Class 2, 4–4–0, 687 on local passenger duties at the south end of the up platform of Macclesfield Central. W. A. Brown collection.

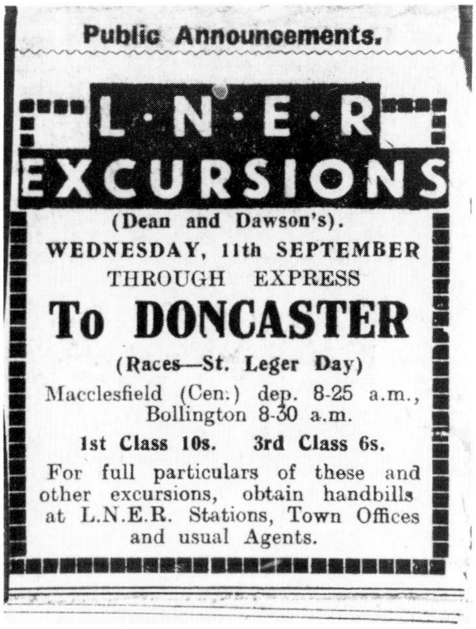

Public Announcements.

L·N·E·R

EXCURSIONS

(Dean and Dawson's).

WEDNESDAY, 11th SEPTEMBER

THROUGH EXPRESS

To DONCASTER

(Races—St. Leger Day)

Macclesfield (Cen.) dep. 8-25 a.m., Bollington 8-30 a.m.

1st Class 10s. 3rd Class 6s.

For full particulars of these and other excursions, obtain handbills at L.N.E.R. Stations, Town Offices and usual Agents.

Newspaper advertisements like this were a regular feature in the Macclesfield paper. This advertisement relates to 1929. Author's collection.

Rose Hill station, c. 1912, looking south. On the right hand side of the end of the down platform can be seen the signal box, built in 1898, as part of a scheme to lengthen the platforms and provide additional siding accommodation. The chimney from Tymm's lime works can be seen in the background. Author's collection.

goods traffic, but carried pigeons between Bollington and Macclesfield on Fridays; although, before coming to Macclesfield, it had hauled an extra passenger trailer, when required, this facility was rarely used when at Macclesfield. In addition to the driver (Bert Jackson was the first driver, who was transferred from Dinting), there was a lad who "looked after the mechanics at the other end", who was paid 19s. 2d. per week for a 6-day/9-hour shift.

The Macclesfield to Buxton passenger excursion workings gradually reduced. From 1908 to 1914, there were 3 trains a day each way on Saturdays in June, July and August and 1 in September. All the trains from Macclesfield stopped at Bollington and the 10.25 a.m. picked up at Poynton; all trains put down at Disley, New Mills, Whaley Bridge, Chapel and Buxton. On the return workings, all trains picked up from Chapel to Disley, set down at Poynton on request on the evening trains, and called at Bollington. The service was suspended after September 1914, and resumed in 1922 from May to September, Saturdays only and 1 train each way; this pattern repeated itself in the summers until 1927 and the scheduled passenger service ended on 3 September 1927 for all time.

Some interesting excursion workings and arrangements are worthy of a brief mention. From 1912 to 1914, on summer Sundays, there was a special excursion to Waterhouses and the Manifold Valley from Bollington and Macclesfield. This train was the 2.20 p.m. from Bollington which stopped at all the intermediate stations down the Churnet Valley line to Leek, formed part of the 3.10 p.m. stopping train from Leek which reached Waterhouses at 3.40 p.m.; arrival at Hulme End was 4.25 p.m. For those passengers who had endured the 2-hour run from Bollington, there was the pleasure of a stay of 90 minutes at Hulme End before the 3-hour return journey to Bollington.

Another interesting excursion was organised by the NS on 26 September 1922 from Macclesfield to the Northern Counties Water Polo Final at Burslem; this was worked by a GC locomotive in the charge of an NS pilot driver, and with an NS guard and NS coaching stock. The Co-operative Wholesale Society organised a "Guaranteed Dining Excursion" for 400 passengers on 26 July 1924 from Macclesfield and Bollington to Marylebone for the Great Exhibition. On 7 July 1928, there were 2 excursion trains from Macclesfield to Knutsford for the Liberal Demonstration, going via Woodley, Stockport and Altrincham; this was an extremely long journey by rail, bearing in mind the road distance was only 12 miles.

In 1915 the CLC continued to offer cycling and walking tours to Macclesfield and Bollington; in 1926 they offered anglers' tickets at 3rd class fares from Manchester (Central) and Chorlton to all stations down the MB&M, and from Warrington (Central) to Poynton, Bollington and Macclesfield. The CLC advertised connections from Liverpool, Warrington and Southport to Macclesfield continued until 1923 with 3 trains each way and an extra train on Saturdays. In 1927 the LNE produced a booklet containing 139 walks in and around Cheshire and Derbyshire; many of these were centred on the stations along the MB&M.

In August 1912, the GC offered the following season ticket facilities on a 1, 3, 6 and 12 months basis – from Macclesfield to all the stations on the MB&M and to Buxton, from Manchester to Rose Hill (3rd class for 12 months £7 16s.), from Manchester to all stations on the MB&M, from Stockport to High Lane, Middlewood, Poynton and Bollington. No clear logic can be deduced from the pattern of these arrangements.

Turning now to goods and mineral traffic, the period from 1907 to 1930 saw many interesting changes. The decline of the railway network of the Poynton Collieries began about 1913 with the closure of Lord and Lady Pits. On 19 March 1920, much of the Poynton Estate was sold off in lots by auction; in 1924 Anson Pit closed and the single line branch to the MB&M fell into disuse. Some coal from Park Pit continued to be sent to the canal via Anson Pit, and some coal was despatched by barge until the 1930's.

This private owner wagon was one of several hundred owned by Poynton Collieries and is seen here newly built. Note the routing instructions, viz via Stockport L&NW and via Woodley GCR. Historical Model Railway Society collection.

Elsewhere, at Rose Hill, in 1909 the Marple UDC was given the first opportunity to purchase the Rose Hill Brick and Tile Works, but it was not until February 1913 that the Council purchased the Works for £2,150. It was from this time that the Council had its own siding at Rose Hill, and for many years it was used by the Council to receive coal for the Gas Works (from the Staffordshire and Yorkshire coalfields in the main) and to receive granite, limestone, tarred slag, and sanitary pipes for road maintenance. The tenders for the Council contracts stipulated a price for delivery to Rose Hill station; contracts, over the years, were awarded, for example, to Pwllheli Granite, Ashton and Holmes (of Macclesfield), and Hartington Quarries, and this business provided regular goods traffic to Rose Hill.

L&NW 19" Goods Class, 4-6-0, 1058, at Macclesfield Central in 1917, and about to reverse into the NS yard. This engine was built at Crewe in July 1908 and withdrawn from service in December 1935. W. Whiston.

Mrs. Arden of Bollington, worked as a goods clerk in Bollington during the first World War and recalls details of goods traffic into Bollington at that time; cotton yarn came into the mills (for example Swindells, Clarence, and Oliver's), paper came in for Henry Leigh Slater, whilst Hammonds of Pott Shrigley brought down wagon loads of brick every night; flour came in by rail from Ashby de la Zouch and was stored at Lowerhouse Mill; yarn was sent to Wardle and Davenports at Leek. The MB&M at Bollington was served by 3 horses drawing carts at that time.

The pattern of goods traffic over the MB&M into Macclesfield from the GC and the CLC in July 1910 consisted of 2 GC goods trains daily from Ardwick, a daily GC pick up from Godley calling at all stations down the branch except High Lane, 2 GC goods (Tuesdays to Saturdays) from Godley to Macclesfield and an extra one on Mondays, a Tuesdays to Saturdays CLC goods from Huskisson, and a daily CLC goods from Heaton Mersey with an extra trip on Saturdays. Into Macclesfield on Sundays was a CLC goods from Heaton Mersey and a GC goods from Godley. Nearly all these trains stopped at Bollington to detach traffic. The daily return workings from Macclesfield were broadly similar. All trains stopped at Bollington to attach traffic, but only the daily Macclesfield to Ardwick stopped to pick up and detach traffic at Poynton and Rose Hill. The daily Macclesfield to Godley also attached traffic at Rose Hill, but otherwise there was no stops for goods traffic at the immediate stations.

The direct express goods between Huskisson and Macclesfield ceased in May 1916 and was never resumed; Liverpool dock traffic for Macclesfield was worked through the daily service to Heaton Mersey. By 1922 the pattern had changed. Into Macclesfield, there was a daily GC goods from Ardwick, a daily GC pick up from Godley calling at all stations down the branch, a daily GC pick up from Dewsnap which called at Rose Hill, Poynton and Bollington, and from Godley to Macclesfield 3 GC goods services on Tuesdays to Fridays with 2 on Mondays and 4 on Saturdays; there was a daily CLC goods from Heaton Mersey and a Guide Bridge to Macclesfield goods on Sundays. Nearly all goods trains called at Bollington. Interesting features of the goods workings from Macclesfield were a Tuesdays to Saturdays Macclesfield to Bollington working, a Saturdays only pilot working to Bollington to shunt the yard, and a strengthening of the service to Guide Bridge – 1 on Mondays, 2 on Tuesdays to Fridays, and 3 on Saturdays; of all the goods workings from Macclesfield, only the daily working to Guide Bridge stopped other than at Bollington, and that only at Rose Hill. There was no return working from Macclesfield to Ardwick though by 1925 this had been restored.

The NS goods working along the MB&M to Middlewood Junction showed very little change between 1907 and 1922; there was an ordinary goods train from Etruria (near Stoke) to Macclesfield and then to Middlewood on a Tuesdays to Saturdays only basis until 1910, when a Monday service was added; traffic was picked up at Bollington and Poynton on the route to Buxton and detached on the way back at Bollington. Traffic was exchanged at Middlewood with goods from Buxton. In 1923, after grouping, the LMS started a Tuesdays to Saturdays goods service from Grange Junction (near Stoke) and Macclesfield, over the Middlewood curve, as far as New Mills and back. By 1929, this had been discontinued and replaced by a through goods working daily from Buxton to Macclesfield, calling at Dove Holes, Whaley Bridge, New Mills and Middlewood Junction, with the return working to Bollington, Poynton (when required) and New Mills.

This fascinating picture, c. 1929, is of a GC/NS horse and cart, the last to survive at Bollington, with a dust-collector built by Wheeldon and Wrigley of Bollington. William Bennett is wearing the apron. A. Wrigley collection.

NS New L Class 0–6–2T, 98, departing from Macclesfield Central with a goods train from the GC/NS exchange sidings for NS lines, c. 1917. W. Whiston.

From the exchange sidings at Macclesfield there were separate daily goods workings in June 1910 down the NS main line to Etruria, Stoke, Sideway, Cliff Vale, and Pratt's Sidings, down the Churnet Valley to Uttoxeter, to Stretton Junction, and to Burton, and down the Biddulph Valley line (via Congleton Lower Junction) to Black Bull (Mondays to Fridays) and to Ford Green (on Saturdays); both the express goods from Manchester to Stoke (Mondays excepted) and the Sundays Longsight to Stoke, which came down the L&NW to Hibel Road, reversed at Central into the exchange sidings. There was a lesser frequency of goods workings into the exchange sidings from the NS main line, though the frequency of return workings from the Biddulph Valley and the Churnet Valley was the same.

The 1924 working timetables show some diversion of the traffic from Sideway, from Stretton Junction, and from the Biddulph Valley line to Hibel Road away from the exchange sidings. In 1929 there was a Tuesdays to Fridays fish and parcels train from Central to Stoke, Fenton and Normacot.

NS 0–6–0T, D Class, on shunting duties in the exchange sidings at Macclesfield, c. 1905. Behind on the left can be seen Lower Heys mill, and on the right the Gas Works. Author's collection.

8 The LNE and LMS Group Committee No. 1 - 1930 to 1947

The first meeting of the LNE and LMS Group Committee No. 1 took place on 11 March 1930 at King's Cross, London. The constitution of the Committee had been determined by section 50 of the London, Midland and Scottish Railway Act of 1924 to supervise the management of 10 undertakings jointly owned by the 2 railway companies; among these joint railways to be managed in this way was the Great Central and North Staffordshire Railway, and the Great Central and Midland Joint Railway (which went through Marple Wharf Junction to New Mills and Hayfield). The Committee was to total 8, 4 from each company, and the quorum was to be 4, 2 from each company. The Chairman for the first year was to be from the LNE, and then from the LMS and LNE alternately; the Chairman did not have a casting vote, and any dispute was to be referred to arbitration. The LNE was to have permanent responsibility for the appointment of a Secretary, and the meetings were to take place at King's Cross at 11 a.m. on the same day in March, June, October and December, as the CLC met. The nominations for the committee from the LNE were G. B. Butler-Henderson, Lord Faringdon (who was to become the first Chairman), W. B. Gair and F. L. Steel, and from the LMS were G. Behrens, C. Booth, Sir Edwin F. Stockton and F. H. Wedgwood; J. McLaren, who had been Secretary to the LNE since 1923, was appointed Secretary to the Committee.

From that time on, the MB&M ceased to be managed as an independent operation as it had been hitherto, although in the past all major decisions had been referred upwards to the General Managers of the respective Parent companies. From 1930 until December 1947 (the last date when Railway Minutes are currently available on the MB&M), the affairs of the MB&M are reported in much less detail in the Minute Books. This information has been supplemented by the recollections of many retired railwaymen who recall well the events of that time.

In the early part of the period from 1930 to 1947, the Committee spent some time reviewing the methods being used for the cartage of goods. In 1929, cartage of goods traffic at Macclesfield had been by 7 horse teams and a chain horse, but because of the increased traffic the LNE had loaned a lorry; this lorry had been able to deliver to districts not previously covered by horses and it was estimated that at least a 3-horse team would be needed to cope with comparable business. The existing motor on loan had a 4-ton capacity and an annual running cost of £660 compared with a cost of £691 for a 3-horse team; it was agreed in October 1931 to purchase a 4-ton AEC motor chassis and cab, with the body being built at LNE workshops. Bollington had been served since 1918 by a motor lorry (in addition to a 3-horse team) which had been withdrawn from service and replaced by a LNE vehicle on loan; in June 1933 approval was given to the purchase of an Albion lorry, with platform body and pneumatic tyres, at a cost of £594. In 1935 Macclesfield and Bollington came under the LNE and LMS pooling scheme which was brought into operation in September 1935 in Macclesfield and in October 1935 in Bollington; after this, there were 3 vans, 16 horse vehicles and 5 horses based at Macclesfield, and 2 horses at Bollington.

In October 1932, approval was given for a 20-ton cart weighbridge at Rose Hill for £311; this followed pressure from Marple UDC, and complaints from traders who were already diverting some traffic to road.

As part of a review of operating costs of the MB&M, detailed plans for singling the branch and for the closure of Hibel Road were

A van of the type used in the Macclesfield area from the 1930's for parcels traffic. Note the front of the van says LMS & LNE and the side LNE & LMS. By courtesy of National Railway Museum, York.

LNE 2-6-0, Class K2, 1739, approaching Middlewood on an up fitted freight on 1 January 1947. This traffic was diverted over the MB&M while the Woodhead line was being electrified. W. J. Skillern.

prepared in 1933. The singling proposals included the conversion to single line north of Bollington and south of Park and Paterson's sidings at Rose Hill, the use of the up platform only at High Lane and the down platform only at Middlewood, the removal of the flyover at Middlewood, the repositioning of the signal boxes at Higher Poynton (to the south end of the up platform) and at Bollington (to the north end of the down platform), and the use of some of the redundant line as extra sidings at Higher Poynton and Bollington. The scheme for the closure of Hibel Road and for the concentration of passenger traffic at Central was more ambitious. A new, wider, bridge was to be built over Buxton road to cater for, on the down, a new bay platform for local traffic to Prestbury, etc. and to Manchester (London Road) and, on the up, 2 extra lines to be put in behind the up buildings so as to convert the up side into an island platform; this would connect with the MB&M and provide goods traffic from the exchange sidings passing on either side of the island platform. Both platforms were to be lengthened significantly, and the terminus of the MB&M was to be the new down platform. These proposals never came to fruition.

The Committee in March 1934 received the financial results for 1933 and it was agreed that the management of both companies should report as soon as possible on the advisability or otherwise of closing the MB&M. The trading performance in recent years had been poor – losses in the 4 years to December 1933 had totalled £62,584 and were a constant financial drain on the respective parent companies. In August 1934, the officers of the LNE and LMS agreed with the report of the management that the line should not be closed because trade was picking up, and the MB&M was given a reprieve – for 35 years! Losses did however continue, all be it at a reduced rate – £5,435 in 1934, £5,587 in 1935, £12,075 in 1937 and £4,767 in 1938 (the last year for which information is available).

Despite the financial difficulties the permanent way programme continued at a heavy rate – in 1934 relaying of 1¾ miles cost £4,062 and re-sleepering of 3¼ miles cost £4,114. Given that gross receipts in 1935 amounted to only £31,778, this expenditure on permanent way is very significant. In 1935, it was reported that the gradual subsidence of the embankment at Middlewood station necessitated the renewal of the timber work and the raising of the platform; various schemes were considered, including rebuilding nearer High Lane, but these were all rejected, and work was approved in October 1936 on the existing station for £1,939.

Mention should be made of the closure of Poynton Collieries on 30 August 1935 when some 250 men were made redundant. In July 1936, Poynton Collieries agreed to the connection with the MB&M being removed and also to relieve the Committee of the obligations under the agreements and understandings of 1864, 1866 and 1888; the net cost to the Committee of lifting its part, 110 yards, of the line to Anson Pit amounted to £118, and this work had been carried out by 30 March 1938. One consequence of this closure was the need for the Chadkirk Print works at Marple to secure its coal from another source, and an additional siding was approved in 1937 at Rose Hill to handle the coal traffic (6,000 tons a year) which would be coming in from the North Staffordshire and South Yorkshire coal fields.

One of the measures taken to reduce operating costs on the MB&M was the closure of the "GC" shed at Macclesfield in November 1935; there had been for many years 6 LNE locomotives shedded at Macclesfield, and since 1921 the petrol electric railcar; there were 4 goods tank engines, one passenger "tank", and a station pilot which also shunted at Bollington and Rose Hill. All the drivers and firemen were transferred to Gorton, where some still live to this very day. In December 1936 part of the roof of the engine shed was blown off, and, in view of its poor condition and lack of suitability for conversion to warehouse use, demolition was approved in 1937.

The last direct link with the NS was severed in July 1937 when C. G. Rose, the Engineer to the MB&M and formerly to the NS, retired; engineering duties were transferred to the Chief Civil Engineer of the LMS, and Stoke Division continued to the responsible for engineering design for many years after that.

In June 1938, it was reported that the storage accommodation at Macclesfield was inadequate, and it was agreed that £2,933 be spent on a new single storey warehouse equipped with a 10 cwt. electric overhead crane; repairing of the goods yard cost a further £610.

Between 1930 and 1940 there were 2 major re-signalling operations. The first, in 1934, involved the closure of the Mortar Mill and Macclesfield Junction signal boxes with the replacement of a new Macclesfield Central signal box. The second, in 1939, involved alterations and additional signalling and track circuiting at Marple Wharf Junction and Rose Hill; this enabled Rose Hill box to be opened for fewer hours with consequent savings in running costs.

Following the outbreak of war in September 1939, it was agreed, in February 1940, that the periodical meetings of the Committee be suspended and during the war-time period the Committee met every February. The war-time period saw the replacement, wherever possible, of male staff by female staff; this started on the MB&M in 1940 when 2 male clerks were replaced by 2 female clerks, and at Middlewood High level box Mrs. G. Parker was appointed as a signalwoman, a position she held until 1946. During the war there were 2 female porters at both Middlewood and Higher Poynton and 1 at High Lane. Also during the war the Poynton signal box was not manned, as an economy measure, and only opened as required; it was not until July 1946 that 3 trainee signalmen were appointed to work round the clock at Poynton box, but they left in 1947 after their training was complete. From November 1946 and over the next few months, the female staff were dispensed with. Permanent way work continued during the war, albeit at a reduced level, but both lines were relaid in the period from 1943 to 1945, with longer sections of rail and steel keys being used. Central station was subjected to major relaying activities in that period, and, in the 4 years ended December 1947, £20,503 was spent on renewal of the permanent way – a significantly higher level than in previous years. The MB&M was upgraded to cope with a substantial number of through freight trains, diverted along the line in 1946 and 1947 during the construction of the Woodhead tunnel. They ran to and from the

LNE, via Egginton Junction. The MB&M was also used for the ballast trains for Woodhead. In June 1947, approval was given for the demolition of the original MB&M station building, built in 1869 at a cost of £828, and which had latterly been used as a shelter for road motor vehicles.

During the period 1930 to 1947 various engineering schemes were prepared but not proceeded with. In 1934 plans were produced to put in a siding for 10 trucks for the Cheshire Brick Company at Middlewood; this was to be achieved by slewing the up line between the Middlewood flyover and the line to Disley. In 1946 plans for the removal of the crossover north of Higher Poynton station were prepared but were not implemented.

The Bollington Bug, the petrol electric railcar, built by the British Westinghouse Electric and Manufacturing Co. Ltd., and purchased by the GC for £2,500 in 1912. It was a small double bogie-car 41′ 6″ long, had fuel tanks for a run of 150 miles, and a maximum running speed of 40 m.p.h. Its colour was teak. It is seen here at Central station, c. 1932. W. A. Brown collection.

Turning now to passenger services, the Bollington Bug still provided 10 services a day each way in 1931 (none on Sundays) including an evening trip as far as Woodley; on Saturdays there was also a late afternoon journey to Higher Poynton (the station name was changed on 13 April 1930 to avoid confusion with the L&NW station of the same name) for shoppers returning from market, and a late evening train for those enjoying a night out in Macclesfield and Bollington; it returned every night for stabling at Macclesfield. The Bug was withdrawn from service in August 1935 and replaced by a Sentinel steam railcar, named "Commerce", which performed the same shuttle duties. For the first few months, this may well have been stabled at the GC shed at Macclesfield, but, after this shed closed in November 1935, the railcar returned every night to Gorton shed. It dropped its last passengers off at Bollington (Poynton on Saturdays) before working through empty stock to Gorton, and in the mornings worked through empty stock to Bollington, arriving 7 a.m. and departing for Macclesfield at 7.23 a.m. The Sentinel was coal fired and firemen who were rostered to work it considered their activities "degrading" as it required so little effort. The Sentinel had a short life on the MB&M, being withdrawn from service in January 1939; after that date the regular shuttle services between Macclesfield and Bollington that had been a feature since August 1921 ceased to be provided. Both the "Bug" and "Commerce" provided 3rd class travel only.

LMS Stanier designed 2-6-4T, 2540, on the down through line at Macclesfield Central 1937. The LNE Sentinel can just be seen behind the down platform awaiting a trip to Bollington. E. R. Morten.

In July 1931, there were 12 daily services on weekdays between Macclesfield and Manchester, 1 extra on Saturdays, and 7 on Sundays; there was also a daily service at 9.45 a.m. between Rose Hill and Manchester for shoppers. There were 13 daily services from Manchester into Macclesfield, 1 extra on Saturdays, and 7 on Sundays, and a daily service, into Rose Hill only, at 9.35 a.m. In July 1939, there was little change in the frequency of service between Macclesfield and Manchester, but between Manchester and Rose Hill had been increased to 4 on Mondays to Fridays, to accommodate the growth of Marple as a commuter suburb. Soon after the outbreak of the Second World War on 3 September 1939 came the introduction, by the LNE, of Emergency Time Tables from 2 October 1939, and, in October 1940, there was a reduction of 3 trains a day each way both between Macclesfield and Manchester and Rose Hill and Manchester; there was no shuttle service between Macclesfield and Bollington – the last such train, which worked on a push and pull basis, was the 4.30 p.m. Saturdays only train to Bollington for market shoppers and this service ended in September 1939. After the war the reductions in service were reinstated and the April 1947 passenger service consisted of 11 trains a day each way between Manchester and Macclesfield, with 2 extra on Saturdays and 6 each way on Sundays; the Manchester to Rose Hill service was 4 trains each way, Mondays to Fridays, and 1 each way on Saturdays.

An N5 working an afternoon local to Manchester across Bollington viaduct in the late 1930's. This viaduct was the major engineering feature on the line. Author's collection.

In the 1930's, Middlewood station was very little used – there was no through service to Stockport, and indeed people from Higher Poynton and Bollington often changed on to the L&NW line at Middlewood to continue to Manchester via the faster route. A few cotton workers from New Mills changed at Middlewood for Bollington, and a few from Macclesfield did the journey the other way. On Tuesdays and Thursdays, the Muffinmen from the bakery at Bollington changed at Middlewood to sell their wares in New Mills, Furness Vale and Whaley Bridge. Middlewood was certainly a lot busier in the summer with day trippers and anglers.

Passenger excursions on the MB&M in the 1930's followed a standard pattern – there were regular excursions every year to Bridlington, Ainsdale Beach and Southport, and Scarborough; these were reduced severely during the war, and in 1940, for example, there was only 1 excursion arranged – during the Macclesfield Barnaby fortnight in June – to Ainsdale Beach and Southport. There was the occasional special excursion from Manchester (Central) to Bollington for visitors to the Salesian College at Pott Shrigley. One incident worthy of note took place on 22 June 1935 when excessive heat caused the rail to buckle on the Marple viaduct – only the vigilance of the driver, Walter Smith, a well-known councillor in Macclesfield, avoided a serious disaster. There were, in the summer months, regular evening excursions from Macclesfield to Buxton at 1s. return.

The freight and goods services on the MB&M followed the standard pattern – services between Macclesfield and Buxton, Godley, Ardwick and Heaton Mersey ran on a daily basis in 1937. Most services called at Bollington and Rose Hill, and the Mondays only Godley to Macclesfield goods train stopped at Middlewood Junction to exchange traffic. The daily pick up was the 1.30 p.m. Godley to Macclesfield, calling at Rose Hill and at Poynton and Bollington if required; this was the only goods train to stop at Poynton for traffic purposes, though most engines stopped to take water. There were no Sunday goods workings. In October 1944, there was a reduced frequency because of the war but the pattern of the service continued; the daily pick-up between Macclesfield and Rose Hill, which did not stop at Poynton, was worked by the GC pilot engine still left at Macclesfield. The LMS daily freight service between Buxton and Macclesfield terminated at New Mills on the return working. The service picked up and dropped off goods at Bibbington's (this traffic started in 1935), Dove Holes, Whaley Bridge, New Mills and Bollington, whilst exchanging the small amount of traffic off the LNE at Middlewood Junction; shunting and traffic exchange also took place there and traffic movements for Railway Clearing House purposes were also recorded.

Freight trains exchanged much of their traffic at the exchange sidings of the MB&M at Macclesfield. Such traffic included coal from Stoke for Yorkshire and Humberside, as well as for the coal depots at Macclesfield, Bollington and Rose Hill, oil tanks from Ellesmere Port, and breakfast items from Kelloggs at Trafford Park. A major impetus was given to the flagging fortunes of the MB&M in the 1930's through the use of Bollington station for the despatch of paints from Barratt Brothers, at Lower House Mill, to Woolworth shops throughout the country. In 1932 £6,205 was received from Woolworth's, £6,749 in 1933 and £7,716 in 1934; this traffic alone accounted for approximately one-third of freight traffic receipts in those years, but ceased in September 1935 when the firm transferred

Former GC 4-4-0, D6 Class, 5859, seen at Rose Hill in the winter of 1940 heading a passenger train to Manchester. Presumably the troops lining the platform have been on snow clearance duty. J. M. Ryan collection.

An unidentified Ivatt-designed former GN 4-4-2T, Class C12, seen here working a Macclesfield to Manchester local, c. 1942 at Middlewood. This view is from the footbridge over the line looking towards Disley. W. J. Skillern collection.

Former GC 0-6-0, J11 Class, 4417, leaving Higher Poynton on 2 June 1946 with a Macclesfield to Manchester local. F. Dean.

to Shrewsbury. Traffic from the GC section detached at Godley included fish from Grimsby, washed slack from the South Yorkshire coalfields, and steel ingots from Birmingham and Rotherham, all for Shelton steelworks at Stoke, and paper from Hull Docks for Backhouse and Coppock at Macclesfield. From Ardwick and from Guide Bridge, in tranship vans, came malt hops for the various Macclesfield breweries, whilst up to 50 wagons at a time brought paper and wicker to the Hovis factory at Macclesfield; competition in Macclesfield for goods traffic was fierce as the respective station masters (LMS from Hibel Road and LNE from Central) canvassed the factories for the trade. From Heaton Mersey came coal for Rose Hill coal merchants and for the Macclesfield Gas Works, and, from Liverpool, via Heaton Mersey, came cotton for the mills in Bollington and Macclesfield, and flour for the Macclesfield bakehouse. Over the Middlewood curve came limestone from the Buxton area, in particular from Bibbington's but also from Miller's Dale, all destined for Shelton. Milk traffic, which for many years had been carried on the 7.20 a.m. Macclesfield to Manchester passenger train, and put off at Hyde, declined due to road competition; it was always loaded at Central station, and 1945 saw the removal of the milk landing stage at the front of the Waters Green entrance of the station.

Exchange traffic in February 1940 from Macclesfield to the former NS network consisted of daily workings to Leekbrook, Uttoxeter, Grange Junction, Horninglow, Sideway and Kidsgrove; daily workings into Macclesfield were from Stoke, Congleton, Sideway and Uttoxeter.

After the war Group Committee meetings reverted back to a quarterly arrangement. The last meeting of the Group Committee took place on 9 December 1947 at Marylebone station, with the Hon. E. B. Butler-Henderson in the Chair, and the end of the MB&M as a separate entity was nigh.

Former GC 4-4-2, C13 Class, 5029, in war-time "NE" livery, at Higher Poynton on 2 August 1943. The signal box still bears the name Poynton even though the name was changed in 1930. Behind the locomotive can be seen the water column. F. Dean.

LNE 0-6-0, J39 Class, 4735, leaving Higher Poynton on 8 June 1947 with a Macclesfield to Manchester local. In the background is the spur to the Poynton Collieries, the track of which was lifted in 1938. F. Dean.

High Lane station battered by snow in the winter of 1947. W. Burton collection.

9 Rundown and Closure Under British Rail – 1948 to 1970

The 1947 Transport Act authorised the state takeover of all heavy land transport, under the aegis of the British Transport Commission, with a Railway Executive to manage the railway system. On 1 January 1948, the LMS, the LNE, the Southern Railway, and the Great Western Railway ceased to exist, and the new state-controlled system was titled British Railways (BR). The Joint Committee of the LNE and LMS, which had managed its affairs and those of several other "joint" railways from 1930 to 1947, was discontinued. For all operating purposes the MB&M had been under the day-to-day control of the LNE (the staffing was controlled from London Road, the District Passenger Manager and Operating Superintendent were based at London Road, whilst the Goods Manager worked from Deansgate, Manchester), though engineering design and control of maintenance remained with the LMS at Stoke, the only legacy of the Knotty origins of the MB&M. The history of the MB&M until nationalisation has relied on the minutes, journals and ledgers (far from complete) of the various Committees which owned and managed it; because the MB&M was integrated into the rest of the railway network, and, because the minutes of BR operating activities are not yet available to the public, information and dates on some aspects may be less than precise.

The period from 1948 to 1970 was sadly one of contraction for the railway network, and from which the MB&M did not escape. In summary, the 1950's saw the run down of freight services and the consequent closure of goods depots down the line in the early 1960's; although the passenger services benefited from the introduction of a diesel service in June 1957, at the expense of an ageing fleet of steam locomotives and stock, this was not enough to stave off the inevitable threat of closure. The closure of Hibel Road station in November 1960, linked to the modernisation of Central station, did not appear to improve the fortunes of the MB&M, and the main line electrification from Manchester to Euston which was introduced, via Macclesfield, in March 1967, did not boost custom down the MB&M because the link was not well-publicised.

In 1963, there appeared the report from the Chairman of the newly-formed British Railways Board, Dr. Beeching, entitled "The Reshaping of British Railways". The main substance of that report was that many of the lesser used lines and stations, for passengers and freight, ran at such a loss as to undermine the profitability of the network as a whole. The MB&M was, from that time on, under threat but managed to survive until January 1970.

Between 1948 and 1970 there were many changes on the MB&M, some following the run down in goods and passenger activities, and some from rationalisation of railway activities at Macclesfield and from electrification. 1949 saw the removal of the GC turntable, which somehow survived after the shed closure in 1935. In 1950, the sidings in the Park and Paterson works at Rose Hill were removed; latterly they had been very little used with traffic increasingly going by road. The track to the private sidings was not removed until 1965.

In 1950 plans were prepared to take out the flyover at Middlewood, to have a single up and down line and to increase siding accommodation from 45 to 97 wagons; these were not proceeded with. At Middlewood High Level Junction, the facing connection from the down line to the curve leading to the Low Level Junction was removed on 17 April 1955, the facing connection from the Low Level Junction from the down line to the curve leading to the High Level Junction having been removed on 14 November 1954. The curve was officially closed to traffic as from 20 February 1955, and the bridge over the Stockport/Disley line removed a few months later. The High Level signal box was closed on 15 December 1958 though the sidings remained in use until late 1963 for storing

Former GC 4-4-2T, C13 Class, 67426, pulling away from Rose Hill to High Lane in the early 1950's. The chimney in the background belongs to Park and Paterson's works, and the siding off the MB&M into the works was located near to the position of the rear coach. A. H. Bryant.

The MS&L Parker-designed 0-6-2T, Class N5, consisted of 129 locomotives, nearly all of which survived until nationalisation in 1948. 9333 is seen here in 1948 on the down line beneath Macclesfield Central signal box. Standing on the engine is driver Frank Blackshaw with Thomas Smith, guard, looking on. R. Dyer.

Demolition of the Middlewood flyover in 1955. This view, looking north to Middlewood and Hazel Grove, shows the spur on the left from the Lower to the Higher Junction. A. H. Bryant.

carriages withdrawn from service; these sidings were not completely lifted until 1966. The Middlewood Low Level Junction signal box stayed open until 3 January 1971.

Following the closure of Middlewood Higher station on 7 November 1960, the buildings and platforms remained for some years, though the buildings were boarded up in September 1961. In January 1962, agreement was reached in principle to let the station to a scout group from Hulme, Manchester, but this was not proceeded with. Following a meeting at Middlewood in January 1965, it was finally agreed in May 1966 to demolish the up platform and to reduce the width of the down platform from 12 feet to 7 feet. The up line was blocked on three successive Sundays in July and August 1966 whilst demolition was carried out.

At Macclesfield, rationalisation led to the closure of Hibel Road station effectively on 7 November though officially on 3 December 1960. The rebuilding of Central station started in January 1960, and the new station was officially opened on 7 November 1960 and named "Macclesfield", a separate through platform for the MB&M being provided on the up side. Electrification of the main line to London, through Macclesfield, was preceeded by re-signalling at Macclesfield, which led to the closure of Macclesfield Central signal box (and other nearby boxes) on 19 March 1965.

The period from 1948 to 1970 saw the run down of goods and freight traffic down the MB&M – part as a result of competition from road transport and part as a result of deliberate policy to concentrate on bulk traffic. In May 1948, there were Mondays to Fridays workings from Macclesfield to Godley and to Ardwick, and the pick up to and from Rose Hill; all of these stopped at Bollington. There was also a Saturdays only working each way between Macclesfield and Guide Bridge. The Godley to Macclesfield working was Mondays to Fridays and the Ardwick to Macclesfield service Tuesdays to Saturdays. "The Cheshireman", between Heaton Mersey and Macclesfield was a Mondays to Saturdays working calling at Rose Hill and Bollington.

The June 1956 working timetables show the workings to Godley and Guide Bridge discontinued by that date, though the workings to and from Heaton Mersey and Ardwick continued; the daily pick up between Macclesfield and Rose Hill operated Mondays to Fridays,

The sad end to the original Central station as demolition and reconstruction takes place in the spring of 1960. M. Dickin.

Former LMS Stanier-designed 2-8-0, 48316, of Heaton Mersey shed, shunting in the goods sidings at Macclesfield in February 1952. Lower Heys mill is in the background, and immediately to the rear of the train is the cabin and ground frame for the sidings. J. Davenport collection.

whilst on Saturdays there was an each way working between Macclesfield and Bollington. The through early morning working from Heaton Mersey to Macclesfield ended in the autumn of 1958, to be replaced by an early morning Heaton Mersey to Godley and Godley to Macclesfield workings; the return through working from Macclesfield to Heaton Mersey continued at least until September 1962.

In September 1952, from the former NS network into Macclesfield, there were daily goods workings from Uttoxeter, Chatterley, Sideway, Longton, Cliff Vale, and from Macclesfield there were daily workings to Stoke, Leek Yard, Uttoxeter, Kidsgrove, Grange Junction. By September 1960, the frequency of workings had reduced with daily workings into the exchange sidings to Leek Yard, Uttoxeter, Stoke and Grange Juction.

By September 1956, there had started what was to become a regular feature – through freight workings over the MB&M, which by-passed the exchange sidings at Macclesfield – and which ultimately were to be the final freight workings. In September 1956, there was the Nottingham (Midland) to Brunswick (Liverpool) freight and the return Brunswick to Spondon; there was also the Warrington to Chaddesden and return which continued until September 1964. In June 1957 there was added a Macclesfield to Copley Hill and return working, a re-direction, because of electrification, of a long-standing service which had gone previously by Stockport, and this ceased in June 1962. A Kidsgrove to Copley Hill goods ran from September 1957 to September 1958. In April 1958, a Stoke-Healey Mills service was introduced and this was the last freight working on the MB&M, lasting until 1967. Starting in September 1958, the Hillhouse to Camden service was routed over the MB&M for a while. From June 1960 to September 1963, the Burton to Atherton working was re-routed over the MB&M. In June 1961 an Oakamoor to Widnes sand train was introduced with a return working from Arpley (Warrington) to Oakamoor; following the closure of the Churnet Valley line for freight workings in June 1964, this traffic was re-directed to form part of the Stoke to Healey Mills train, sand traffic being detached at Guide Bridge. In June 1962, a Bescot – Healey Mills service was introduced, and this ran until January 1965.

In the meantime, closure of the various facilities for goods along the MB&M was occurring – on 12 August 1963 the exchange sidings at Macclesfield were closed, to be followed by Bollington goods yard on 7 October 1963. The exchange sidings were used by the Electric Traction Engineer for stabling electrification equipment until 31 August 1965, and the ground frame that worked these sidings was taken out of use on the same date; these sidings and the shunters cabin in the GC yard were cleared by March 1966. The coal yard at Macclesfield closed on 20 September 1969 and the goods yard just over a month later on 30 October 1969, though the goods warehouse had been demolished in 1968.

At Bollington, alternative goods facilities were provided – less than a wagon load to Heaton Norris, and a wagon load to one consignee to Macclesfield. In November 1964 the connections to the

Former GC 0-6-2T N5 Class, 69347, working an up freight to Macclesfield on 24 August 1950. The station nameboard is to a standard NS design and the station changed its name in 1951. N. Fields.

sidings were taken out of use, and the track was lifted in the autumn of 1965. The signal box closed on 18 December 1966, though it had only been open for some years for the shunting of the goods yard. Demolition of the stables, warehouse, and signal box took place early in 1967.

In July 1963, the future of Rose Hill as a goods depot was being considered; on 20 February 1964 approval was given for the depot closure and this finally took place on 26 April 1965. Alternative arrangements were for wagon load traffic to go to New Mills East, coal class traffic to Woodley, and less than a wagon load to Heaton Norris. The last steam train to call at Rose Hill was hauled by a Stanier 2–8–0 in March 1965. Removal of track in the redundant sidings took place in the summer of 1966 and a timber cabin was demolished in January 1967.

At Higher Poynton the signal box closed on 18 December 1966. The water columns were demolished on 19 January 1967 and later sold as scrap. The box was demolished in May 1967 and the crossover removed at that time.

LMS Fowler 2–6–4T, of Longsight shed, in Bollington yard with a mixed freight in 1953. The goods warehouse is on the left. Don West is on the footplate and Francis Roach stands guard. R. Dyer.

A view from the footplate of Marple Wharf Junction box in 1953 of former LMS Fowler-designed 0–6–0, 44500, of Stoke shed, at the head of a Nuneaton to Woodhead ballast train. This ballast train has previously worked over the MB&M before being turned at Godley. Note the sharpness of the curve to the right which is the start of the MB&M. R. Dyer.

▲ *Former GC 0-6-0, 65200, J10 Class, is seen here working back a Godley to Heaton Mersey goods past Bredbury Junction on 24 April 1957. This Class was the mainstay of Cheshire Lines goods working for very many years, including the daily trips to Macclesfield.* W. A. Brown.

◀ *Former LMS Stanier-designed 2-8-0 48094, on a train of fitted sand wagons being returned to Oakamoor, passing Middlewood on 2 June 1962. A single length of track is all that is left of the junction with the Middlewood curve.* J. W. Sutherland.

BR Britannia Class 4-6-2, 70024, "Vulcan" entering the re-modelled Macclesfield station in late 1964, with a goods train from the MB&M, framed by the Macclesfield Central and the new Macclesfield signal boxes. M. Welch.

British Railways designed 2-6-0, 76048, passing Middlewood Higher at 10.20 a.m. on an up goods on 2 June 1962. J. W. Sutherland.

Between 1948 and 1970 there were no significant variations in passenger services, as the following table shows:

May 1948	Dec. 1955	Sept. 1960	May 1969
MANCHESTER TO MACCLESFIELD			
7 daily	9 daily	8 daily	7 daily
5 sat only	4 sat only	6 sat only	6 sat only
4 sat exc	2 sat exc	7 sat exc	7 sat exc
7 sunday	6 sunday	8 sunday	—
MANCHESTER TO ROSE HILL			
1 daily	1 daily	1 daily	1 daily
3 sat exc	3 sat exc	2 sat exc	2 sat exc
MACCLESFIELD TO MANCHESTER			
8 daily	9 daily	11 daily	9 daily
4 sat only	4 sat only	3 sat only	4 sat only
2 sat exc	1 sat exc	3 sat exc	5 sat exc
6 sunday	6 sunday	8 sunday	—
ROSE HILL TO MANCHESTER			
1 daily	1 daily	2 daily	1 daily
3 sat exc	3 sat exc	2 sat exc	2 sat exc

In 1948 there was a late train, 10.20 p.m. from Manchester which went to Rose Hill, High Lane, and Higher Poynton. On 25 July 1951, 72 years after opening, the two stations at Middlewood received separate names – Middlewood Higher and Middlewood Lower. The dieselisation of the passenger service in June 1957 did not lead to any variation in service of significance. The Sunday service was withdrawn on 16 September 1962, even though reputedly the line was busiest on a Sunday when anglers and ramblers travelled from Manchester. After the Manchester to London electrification in 1967, fares to Manchester along the MB&M were raised above those of the line via Prestbury. The final passenger timetable, covering the period from 5 May 1969 to 3 May 1970, showed that approximately three-quarters of the passenger services between Manchester and Macclesfield were via the slower route through Hyde, rather than the quicker route through Bredbury and Reddish; traffic was being squeezed off despite the frequency of service.

Former GC 2-4-2T, E7111, designed by Pollitt for the MS&L in 1896, is seen here at Macclesfield (Central) in 1948. This F2 Class of locomotive, all ten of which were built in 1898 by Beyer Peacock, survived until 1947 and all were withdrawn from service by 1950. This Class ceased to work on the MB&M in the mid-1930's, and this locomotive from King's Cross is on a rare working to Macclesfield after repairs at Gorton. This locomotive was never renumbered in BR days, and the prefix E denotes Eastern Region. Author's collection.

Former GC 0–6–0, J11 Class, 64440, at Rose Hill, c. 1950, working a local passenger to Macclesfield. The signal box was the northern-most of North Staffordshire design replacing the original one on the other platform in 1898.
R. A. Gee.

Former GC 4–4–2T, Class C14, 67444 at High Lane on 25 May 1957, working 12.15 p.m. Saturdays only Manchester (London Road) to Macclesfield local. Behind the station building on the right is the tip from the former King Coal pit. The wooden sign for the Booking and Waiting Hall is of standard NS design.
R. Keeley.

Former LNE Class L1, 2–6–4T, 67795 working a Manchester to Macclesfield local, arriving at Central station in 1955. M. Welch.

The MB&M did however fulfil an important role as a diversionary route in the late 1950's – both for traffic at holiday periods and for traffic diverted off the London to Manchester main line because of electrification. From July 1958 until November 1959, there were frequent passenger workings over the MB&M to and from Manchester (both London Road and Central) and Euston, Birmingham, Northampton, Coventry, Gloucester, and parcel workings to and from Stafford and Manchester (Victoria). On various Sundays in June 1964, and January and February 1965, Manchester to Birmingham trains were sent via the MB&M because of electrification. Special holiday and other excursions over the MB&M included frequent workings between Cheadle (Staffordshire), Bythe Bridge, and Nottingham and Belle Vue over the years; the last Blythe Bridge working to Belle Vue was in March 1967. One of the last passenger excursions over the MB&M was from Walsall to Belle Vue on 17 May 1969. There were occasional passenger excursions between Macclesfield and Buxton over the Middlewood curve – normally for the local football "derby" matches; the last of these excursions took place in 1954.

The first day of diesel working, 17 June 1957, with a Derby light weight 2-car set dmu at Middlewood Higher working to Macclesfield. W. J. Skillern.

This 1954 rear view of the small waiting room on the down platform at Middlewood Higher shows the vulnerability of the station to slippage and subsidence. Note the chimney of the brickworks in the rear. A. H. Bryant.

A view from the same position on 6 October 1956 shows a battered looking former GC 4-6-2T, A5 Class, 69805 on a Macclesfield to Manchester local. Following a landslip, c. 1955, the waiting room was lost and not replaced. W. A. Brown.

A 2-6-4T coming off the flyover at Middlewood towards Buxton with a football special to Buxton on 18 August 1951. In the background on the left can be seen the Middlewood Low Level Junction Box and the curve to the MB&M. E. R. Morten.

The first passenger station on the MB&M to be considered for closure was Middlewood Higher, never well-patronised. The increase in private car ownership and the lower bus fares took a lot of traffic off the railways, and the station, situated three-quarters of a mile from Higher Poynton and half a mile from High Lane and serving a scattered village population of 800, was particularly vulnerable. About 1955 part of the embankment collapsed, taking the down platform with it; instead of being rebuilt, the waiting room was not replaced, and the platform was cut short to accommodate about 3 coaches. Under the Nationalisation Act of 1947, before any line or passenger station could be closed, the Transport Users' Consultative Committee (TUCC), the railway consumers' protection body, was charged with the task of holding a public enquiry to assess the hardship caused by the closure and to report to the Minister of Transport who would decide on the closure. A TUCC meeting took place on 28 March 1960 when it was reported that 71 people joined and 73 alighted at the station on Mondays to Fridays (nearly half of whom were school children going from Disley to Macclesfield) and 34 and 30 on Saturdays. A Committee of Enquiry followed on 10 May 1960 at the Midland Hotel, Manchester, with the objectors putting alternative proposals to reduce costs by rationalisation of the staff between the two stations. With no possibility of increasing traffic, and with further substantial expenditure needed to renew the wooden platform, even the TUCC could not support the case for keeping the station open – and so with a net saving of £507 per annum forecast from the closure, Middlewood Higher closed on 7 November 1960.

The closure notice for Middlewood Higher station, to take effect from 7 November 1960. R. Hughes.

Following the Beeching Report, the London Midland Region of the British Railways Board prepared in July 1965 detailed proposals for the withdrawal of passenger train services between Manchester Piccadilly and Macclesfield and Hayfield via Guide Bridge and via Bredbury.

In arriving at their estimates of financial savings, BR drew up detailed proposals for redundancies. These included the Station Master at Rose Hill (who also had responsibility for High Lane, Higher Poynton and Bollington), a Booking Clerk at Rose Hill, and 9 Leading Porters and Porters from the 4 stations; no changes were proposed for Macclesfield. The 2 permanent signalmen at Rose Hill were to go and the vacancy at Higher Poynton was not to be filled; Bollington box was not manned by this time. On the permanent way, the Rose Hill, Higher Poynton and Bollington gangs (each of 3 men) were to be redundant and the Macclesfield gang was to be reduced by 1. Parcels traffic, both for collection and for delivery, was to be re-arranged – Rose Hill, High Lane and Higher Poynton were to be handled through Stockport Edgeley, Bollington parcels already being dealt with through Macclesfield. Even while these proposals were being considered internally by BR, other plans were being brought forward in January 1966 for a possible chord line through the GC yard which would link the MB&M with the former L&NW line. These plans could well have boosted the fortunes of the MB&M had they been implemented, but it was not to be.

These 1965 proposals formed the background to the financial statement submitted on 30 December 1966 by the Divisional Manager, Manchester, to the Chairman and Members of the North Western Area TUCC for the proposed withdrawal of services between Romiley and Macclesfield. This financial statement showed that estimated earnings per annum from the MB&M amounted to £20,100, and estimated direct costs to £109,500; in addition, renewal on permanent way and signalling for the 5 years to 1971 was estimated to be £48,000. The reduction of income generated by freight traffic after 1948 had undermined the viability of the MB&M, and had threatened its continued existence as a passenger line for some years. These proposals were publicised by the TUCC on 7 January 1967 with users being invited to lodge objections no later than 18 February; it was stated that in the event of no objections, the service would be discontinued on 6 March 1967. Even though it was inevitable that these proposals would cause hardship, BR did not propose the strengthening of any alternative rail services on nearby lines at Macclesfield, New Mills (Central) and Poynton; it did bring forward proposals for the North Western Road Car Company to provide, firstly, a peak hour morning and afternoon bus service for scholars between Romiley and Macclesfield, and additional bus feeder services between Rose Hill and Marple.

BR had carried out passenger surveys on an average weekday in each of July 1965, December 1965 and May 1966. These showed a reasonably steady pattern of approxiamtely 950 journeys a day each way, of which nearly 700 travelled on the section between Rose Hill and Manchester and the remainder on the section from Macclesfield to Rose Hill; the average numbers travelling on Saturdays and the pattern of travelling was the same as for weekdays. The surveys showed that approximately 80% of the journeys started or ended at Macclesfield or at Rose Hill, split equally between the 2 stations, with passenger usage at the intermediate stations accounting for relatively little – the daily average at High Lane was 35, Poynton 80 and Bollington 78. Given the large numbers of passengers likely to be affected, it was inevitable that there would be a loud public outcry, and the TUCC lodged its Points of Objection to BR's Divisional Manager on 3 March. BR had in the meantime given formal notice in accordance with Section 56(7) of the Transport Act 1962 to close the line between Marple Wharf Junction and Macclefield and all the stations, and at the same time the line between New Mills (Central) and Hayfield (involving the closure of Birch Vale and Hayfield stations).

The points that the TUCC raised in opposition to the closure were formidable – the alternative services being offered were inadequate and involved increased travelling time and costs, an issue that BR was prepared to concede; the proposed feeder service between Rose Hill and Marple would create a new traffic hazard; the additional bus services between Romiley and Macclesfield would take 2½ times longer; the reduction in train services between Marple and St. Pancras would increase the necessity of the link the MB&M would provide to the electrified service from Macclesfield to London; the continued existence of the MB&M would widen the job opportunities of Marple residents in Bollington, Macclesfield and Alderley Edge, following the mill closures in Marple; 95 scholars to the King's School and the Girls' High School, Macclesfield, would be affected; considerable residential development was being planned along the line; road congestion would increase, producing an overload on the A6 and a bottleneck at Hazel Grove; walkers to the Peak National Park and anglers to the canals would find travelling difficult; hospital visitors to Macclesfield would find travelling extremely difficult and virtually impossible in the evenings.

The Enquiry in Public was held by the TUCC at the Town Hall, Macclesfield on 31 March 1967. In addition to the detailed arguments of the TUCC's "Points", a petition from Bollington with 361 signatures was presented; the number of objectors who had filled in the official TUCC card totalled 481, of which 239 were from Rose Hill and a mere 15 from Macclesfield, and further individual objectors totalled 493. 31 organisations opposed the closure, but not, significantly, the Macclesfield Borough Council. The TUCC report to the Minister found that the withdrawal of service would cause varying degrees of hardship, particularly to commuters, school children and hospital visitors. The report concluded that the alternative services suggested did not meet the needs of the community, and that if it had been possible to retain 2/3 trains between Rose Hill and Manchester to serve commuters in the morning and evening peaks, then this would have removed the bulk of objectors.

After two years of pondering, the Minister of Transport finally decided on 12 June 1969 to consent to the closure between Rose Hill and Macclesfield, but to reprieve the section between Marple Wharf Junction and Rose Hill. The Minister did attach certain conditions to the closure – that additional or re-timed buses be made available by the National Bus Company on school days only from Rose Hill, High Lane and Poynton stations, that an additional early morning train be provided on weekdays, leaving Macclesfield at 6.25 a.m. via Stockport to Manchester. In reaching his decision the Minister "noted" revised proposals from BR to provide 19 trains daily Mondays to Fridays and 16 trains on Saturdays from Manchester to Rose Hill and 17 trains daily Mondays to Fridays and 15 trains Saturdays in the other direction. The Minister also announced that, because of the social need, he would consider grant-aiding the service between Manchester and Rose Hill under powers contained in Section 39(1) of the Transport Act 1968.

In July, Bollington UDC registered their continued opposition but to no avail. On 28 November 1969, C. P. Millard, the Divisional Manager of BR's London Midland Region, wrote to the North Western TUCC, stating that the closure of Birch Vale, Hayfield, Bollington, High Lane and Higher Poynton stations would be implemented with effect from 5 January 1970. The last northbound train on the line was 10.31 p.m. from Macclesfield on Saturday 3 January. A 2-car dmu, it contained 31 passengers of whom about 15 were local railway enthusiasts, and the remainder were railwaymen and residents, some of them paying a farewell visit to the railway. A ship bell was tolled at each station, accompanied by a fanfare on the diesel's horn.

One passenger was equipped with a red flag which he waved at each station; a union jack was fixed to a window, accompanied by one passenger's written protest – "We want Millard's Blood". The platform at Bollington was unlit and deserted, except for a local newspaper photographer. The sounding of detonators accompanied the train's departure from High Lane where a solitary oil lamp provided the illumination.

The closure notice for the line from Rose Hill to Macclesfield, to take effect from 5 January 1970. R. Hughes.

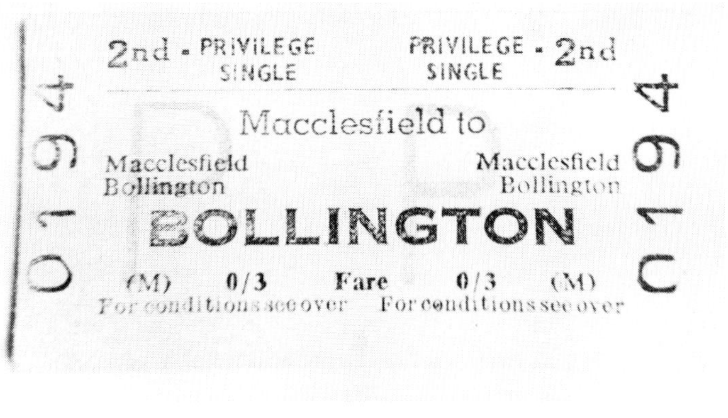

A ticket issued for the last journey on 3 January 1970. R. Dyer.

The final southbound train, also a 2-car dmu, left Romiley 2 minutes late at 11.37 p.m. with 80 passengers aboard. The majority of these were local residents who had spent the evening in Manchester; several others were residents making a farewell journey, and about 20 were railway enthusiasts. The bell and horn were worked in concert to wake the neighbourhood at each station, and detonators were let off at High Lane and Bollington. High Lane and Higher Poynton were used by just a few passengers. Bollington station came to life – part of the platform was lit, and many of the 20 departing passengers stayed to wave the train off. 46 passengers continued to Macclesfield, and front and rear horns worked continuously to mark the end of the passenger service on the MB&M. Arrival at 6 minutes past midnight was only 3 minutes late. After several passengers had sung "Auld Lang Syne" and said their last farewells to the railway staff, the empty coaches returned, via Prestbury, to Manchester . . .

Bollington station has a forlorn look as a 2-car diesel multiple unit leaves for Macclesfield on the last day, 3 January 1970. The goods warehouse and the signal box have already gone, and the station buildings were demolished in 1971.
M. Welch.

10 The Line is Re-born - 1970 to 1983

The closure of the railway line between Rose Hill and Macclesfield is not, however, the end of the story. Early in 1970, a deputation headed by Dr. Michael Winstanley, the M.P. for the Cheadle Constituency (which included Marple and High Lane) obtained an assurance from BR that the MB&M would be kept *in situ* until August whilst the South East Lancashire North East Cheshire Passenger Transport Executive (SELNEC), the authority responsible for providing bus and rail passenger services in the Greater Manchester Conurbation, considered whether they wished to re-open the line; this in reality was a forlorn hope because the section of line between High Lane and Macclesfield was outside the SELNEC area anyway.

In May 1970, a group of railway enthusiasts and other interested people formed a "Lyme Handley Railway Preservation Society" in a vain attempt to save the line; they took their name from the nearby village of Lyme Handley, which incidentally was not on the route. Their immediate objective was to prevent BR lifting the track, and then raise the £50,000 – £100,000 necessary to purchase the line and equipment to operate it. The longer term objective was to single the line, to run a regular diesel railcar service from Rose Hill to Macclesfield during the week, and to provide steam-hauled trains for enthusiasts at weekends. A public meeting in Marple Bridge was held in June 1970, but, despite extensive leafleting in the area, the public support was not forthcoming. Indeed only £300 could be raised, against the £1,400 requested by BR as compensation for not lifting the track, and the scheme failed; the fact that travellers from Rose Hill had an improved service didn't help the objectors. Immediately following the closure, plans were prepared on 16 January 1970, for the removal of the lines in the Macclesfield coal and goods yard. In February 1970, it was agreed that the lifting of these sidings should take place after the lifting of the branch to enable the sidings to be used for wagon stabling whilst the line was being removed.

July 1970 saw the completion of the reconstruction of Rose Hill station, which involved the demolition of the buildings on the up platform, the adaptation of the former ladies' waiting room as a booking office, and replacement of gas lamps with electric lighting. On 6 September, Rose Hill signal box was closed (the only other signal box on the MB&M, Macclesfield Goods Junction, having been closed on 5 January on the closing of the line), and was demolished by the end of the year. Automatic spring points were installed at the crossover south of the station to cross trains; the crossover north of the station was disconnected though not removed. Lifting of the disused line began at Rose Hill on 12 December 1970, reached Bollington by February 1971, and was completed in the spring. The station buildings at Poynton were demolished in the spring of 1971, and those at Bollington by December 1971; High Lane station buildings lasted until 1977 in a ramshackled condition, when they were demolished. At Middlewood, where the Low Level station still exists, a new footpath and footbridge had been built to the up platform on the Buxton line by 1978 when no traces of the former wooden platforms and buildings survived.

At Rose Hill, major alterations took place in 1977 and 1978, involving the erection of a modern ticket booth near the exit gate of the up platform, the modernisation of the car park to provide good road/rail interchange facilities, and the re-siting of Bowden's coal yard; it was not until 27 July 1980 that the line from just south of Marple Wharf Junction to Rose Hill was singled, as part of a re-signalling operation which involved the closure of the signal box at the Junction at the same time.

In March and April 1981, the demolition of the viaduct over the River Bollin at Macclesfield took place, the work being carried out by T. J. Stafford Ltd., of Ardwick, as part of a landscape improvement scheme financed by the Department of Environment. During the demolition it was possible, when the girders were being removed, to assess all the engineering and construction difficulties associated with constructing a railway line which straddled a river.

Demolition of the railway viaduct over the River Bollin at Macclesfield, which took place in March 1981, revealed interesting construction and design features. Macclesfield Express.

A feasibility scheme for the re-use of the line was prepared in 1979 by the Civic Trust for the North West and this led, in June 1982, to detailed proposals for the reclamation for recreational purposes, of the disused railway line from Macclesfield to Middlewood, coming before the Macclesfield Borough Council (MBC). Facilities for recreation were to be made available for pedestrians, cyclists and horseriders, with a footpath along the whole length of line from the Hurdsfield part of Macclesfield to Middlewood. The section of line from Rose Hill to Middlewood is in the geographical area of the Stockport Metropolitan Borough Council (SMBC) and was subject to separate proposals of a similar nature. A joint scheme by SMBC and the Greater Manchester Council for the erection of a gymkhana on the site of the Middlewood Tip provided a logical development to horse riding facilities. The controversial feature of the MBC proposals was the exclusion of the Bollington Viaduct from the scheme, and the request by BR to demolish it. From the start the scheme had its critics – from Poynton about the effect on the inhabitants of extra traffic and from Bollington about the intrusion of horse boxes on car parks. There was a strong lobby in Bollington for the retention of the viaduct, and at a crowded meeting in August at the Civic Hall a petition was launched to save it.

This defiant sign was hung by Bollington residents in August 1982 from the Bollington viaduct in protest against the Macclesfield Borough Council's plans to demolish the viaduct. Macclesfield Express.

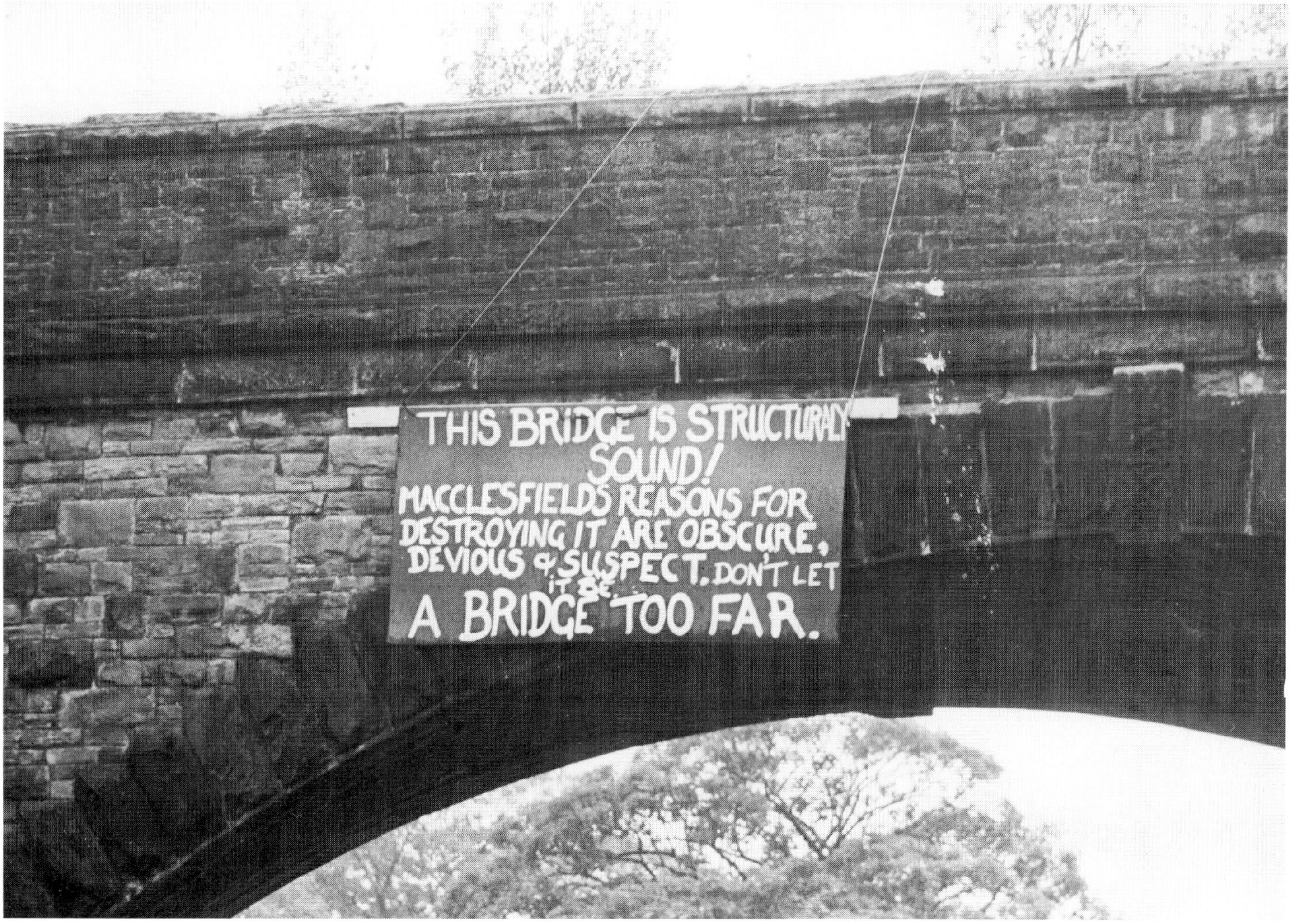

In October 1982, MBC were informed that the Department of Environment had agreed to save the Bollington Viaduct and to include it in the scheme; of the total cost of £600,697 of the Macclesfield Borough section, £571,697 was to come in the form of derelict land grant with the remainder coming from the ratepayers. MBC paid £1 to BR for their $7\frac{1}{2}$ mile section of line and SMBC £10,000 for their $2\frac{1}{2}$ mile section. It is worth noting that the cost of reclaiming the Macclesfield to Middlewood section is nearly double the cost of building it 115 years ago. But the line has a future, and will no doubt contribute to the well-being of the community in the years ahead, as it did in years gone by.

Appendix

APPENDIX I

Officers of the Macclesfield, Bollington and Marple Railway.

ENGINEERS

1863 - 1864	J. I. Mawson (to the Promoters for the Bill)
1865 - 1881	C. R. Sacré; J. C. Forsyth (Joint Engineers)
1881 - 1886	C. R. Sacré
1886 - 1890	W. H. Stubbs
1890 - 1914	J. Crosbie-Dawson
1914 - 1921	F. A. L. Barnwell
1921 - 1937	C. G. Rose

From 1886 the Engineers were from the NS, and its successor, the LMS; all appointees received an honorarium.

After 1937 there ceased to be a separate Engineer for the Railway, the engineering duties being initially transferred to the Chief Civil Engineer, LMS, and later to British Rail.

SECRETARY

1865 - 1892	E. Ross
1893 - 1918	O. S. Holt
1918 - 1923	J. A. Campbell
1923 - 1938	J. McLaren
1938 - 1942	P. J. Dowsett
1943 - 1947	W. H. Johnson

Since 1930, the post was Secretary to the LNE and LMS Group Committee No. 1.

AUDITORS

There were frequent changes but, until 1923, the NS and MS&L (GC) each provided one auditor.

After the "Grouping" of 1923, the LNE assumed responsibility for the appointment of the Secretary and the Auditor. From 1929, accountancy duties were transferred from the Secretary to the Chief Accountant of the LNE.

Extract from MS&L roster, 4 February 1886, for locomotives, drivers and firemen. Note the dotted line showing the route that the locomotive was diagrammed to work. Manchester Central Reference Library.

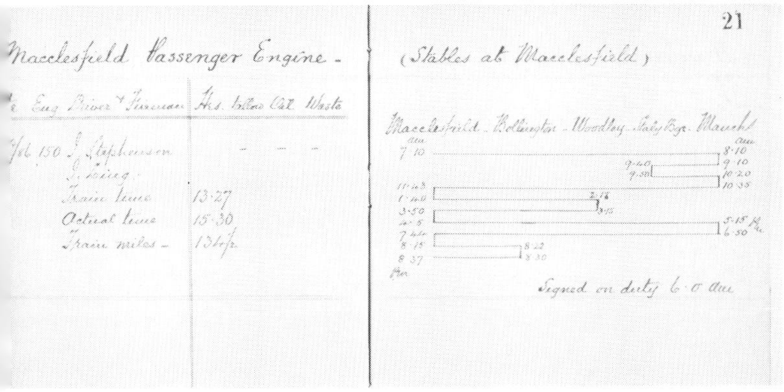

APPENDIX II

Locomotives over the MB&M.

During the years a large number of different locomotive types have worked over the MB&M, and a representative selection of photographs is contained elsewhere in this book. In addition, further information on locomotives has been obtained from published information, library material, personal observations and records, and the detailed recollections of many railwaymen. This section of the book is based on this material which has been pieced together from a wide variety of sources.

The locomotives that worked over the MB&M from the early years down to the end of steam working in the early 1960's reflected, as far as the MS&L and its successor railway companies are concerned, the pool of locomotives, both for local passenger and local freight workings, that were available at the MS&L, etc. depot at Gorton. The MC shed at Macclesfield, from its opening in 1873 down to its closure in 1935, did not have an allocation of its own, but used locomotives that Gorton provided. The MS&L roster of 4 February 1886 shows one passenger engine, 2–4–0, Class 1C, based at Macclesfield whilst another of the same Class based at Gorton worked a passenger service to and from Macclesfield. This Class was built in 1864 and was withdrawn from service between 1902 and 1904. Another passenger engine, 2–4–0, Class 8, was also rostered in February 1886 for the Macclesfield passenger duties; this Class was built in 1871 and scrapped in 1903.

In the early 1890's, these older types were replaced on the line by Parker-designed 2–4–2T, Class 3 (later LNE Class F1), 39 of which were built between 1889 and 1893 for the growing local services in the Manchester area. These engines were mainly responsible for working the passenger services on the MB&M until the mid-1930's when they were gradually replaced by the larger Robinson-designed 4–4–2T, LNE Class C13. This Class then became the regular motive power for passenger workings until withdrawal began in the mid-1950's. Another Class, designed by Pollitt and built in 1898, 9G which later became LNE Class F2, also occasionally saw service on the line. Mention has been made of the Westinghouse petrol electric railcar, the Bollington Bug, which saw service from 1921 to 1935, and of the Sentinel steam car "Commerce" which operated from 1935 to 1939 (being occasionally replaced by another Sentinel, "Rising Sun"); "push-pull" working when required on this service were by F1's until the mid-1930's, and by F2's subsequently until September 1939.

An unusual local passenger working took place in 1936 with the use on the Manchester to Macclesfield run of a Robinson-designed 4–6–0, Class B9 (former GC Class 8G), though this Class was used regularly to work passenger excursions from Macclesfield, Hayfield, and Glossop to Southport and Liverpool.

Former GN Ivatt-design 4–4–2T's, Class C12, were allocated from 1939 to Trafford Park, and worked local passenger services, occasionally down the MB&M.

From 1935 to 1937 on excursion workings from the Potteries and Uttoxeter to Belle Vue (over the MB&M), a mixture of motive power was used, all of Stoke shed; these included Hughes/Fowler 2–6–0's, Stanier 2–6–2T's and 2–6–4T's, and Fowler 0–6–0's.

In BR days, a wide variety of motive power was used on passenger trains. These included Robinson-designed Class J11 0–6–0's which regularly worked some rush hour trains. LNE-built Class J39 0–6–0's saw service in the late 1940's, whilst in the early 1950's Robinson-designed Class C14 4–4–2T engines were brought in. Large engines came in the mid to late 1950's when some of the Robinson-designed Class A5 4–6–2T's and the more modern LNE-designed L1 2–6–4T's were transferred to Gorton and worked on the suburban service from Manchester to Macclesfield, Hayfield and Glossop. From the Macclesfield end, Fowlers 2–6–4T's were introduced in the early 1950's and worked regular passenger turns. June 1957 saw the introduction of diesel multiple units (Derby lightweights) and steam traction was phased out entirely over the next 3 years. DMU's provided the traction until the end of the MB&M in January 1970, and down to the present day on the truncated section from Marple Wharf Junction down to Rose Hill.

Around 1910, a Uttoxeter excursion was worked by 4–4–0 Robinson-designed GC Class 11B (later LNE Class D9); also used on such excursions over the years were Robinson-designed 4–4–0 "Director" Class (GC Class 11E, later LNE Class D10) and "Improved Director" Class (GC Class 11F, later LNE Class D11), "Sir Sam Fay" Class (GC Class 1, later LNE Class B2), and LNE-designed J39 0–6–0's.

Turning now to freight workings over the MB&M, the 1886 MS&L roster shows 3 locomotives allocated for freight duties, all Class 18; these particular locomotives were built between 1870 and 1873, and were scrapped between 1903 and 1909. The short freight trips over the MB&M were worked for the best part of 60 years by Parker-designed N5 Class; this Class of 0–6–2T was built in the period from 1891 to 1901, nearly all survived until BR days, and were withdrawn from service throughout the 1950's. Ivatt-designed former GN 0–6–0 J1's were seen on freight duties at Macclesfield in late 1941 and early 1942.

The CLC freight workings from Huskisson Dock from 1900 to 1916, and subsequent workings from Heaton Mersey until the mid-1920's, were by Sacré-designed 0–6–0 Class 6c (later LNE Class J12); from then until the late 1950's, the CLC working from Heaton Mersey was by Parker-designed 0–6–0, Class J10, but on the withdrawal of the Class in the 1950's LMS Stanier 2–8–0's and BR 2–6–0's were used. The special workings when trains were diverted from the Woodhead route in 1946 and 1947 were, in the main, operated by J11's, and by Gresley-designed former GN 2–6–0 locomotives of Class K2.

From the turn of the century, on the North Staffordshire side, Adams' L Class Vulcan 0–6– 2T and Longbottom's DX Class 0–6–2T provided the motive power on the freight workings to Middlewood and, for a few years until this working from Macclesfield ceased in the mid-1920's, Adams' New L Class 0–6–2T was also used. This Class also worked at this time the passenger services and excursions from Macclesfield to Buxton until the mid-1930's, after which Fowler 2–6–4T's were used for excursion traffic until the early 1950's when workings ceased.

There is little recorded of L&NW activity over the MB&M from Buxton. For a few years until the First World War the passenger workings into Macclesfield were by Precursor 4–4–2T locomotives; the freight workings into Middlewood until the mid-1920's and into Macclesfield after then were in the main hauled by former L&NW G Class and G1 Class 0–8–0 engines, but also in later years, until the working ended in 1946, by former Midland Railway Fowler-designed 0–6–0's.

In BR days the types of locomotives working the through freight over the MB&M were numerous. The trains from the Stoke area to Healey Mills and Copley Hill were worked in the main by Stanier 4–6– 0's Class 5, and in "diesel" times by Class 24's or Class 25's, double-headed. The Brunswick to Spondon workings were by Fowler 4F 0–6–0's. The Widnes to Oakamoor sand trains were worked by Stanier 2–8–0's. The Nuneaton to Woodhead ballast trains were mostly worked by 0–6–04F's, with the occasional Class 5's, and 2–6–0 Fowler "Crabs". As the run-down of steam gathered pace in the early 1960's, even 4–6–2 "Britannias" were seen on humble freight duties.

One unusual working over the MB&M was the Macclesfield to Cornbrook sidings general freight working from April to November 1949; Fowler 0–6–0 4F, 44349, was allocated to Hibel Road shed for this purpose.

APPENDIX III

Mileage Rate Charges

Charges made by MS&L and GC for engine working.

			Per mile
12 August 1869	– 17 November 1873		1s. 1d.
18 November 1873	– 19 May 1874		1s. 4d.
20 May 1874	– 31 December 1876		1s. 2d.
1 January 1877	– 1906		1s. 1d.
Agreement reached October 1921			
Passenger train miles			
Engine power		2s. 9d.	
Coaching stock		6d.	
			3s. 3d.
Petrol electric car			2s. 4d.
Goods train miles			3s. 11d.
Ballasting			21s. per hour
Shunting			21s. per hour

Arm band used by porters engaged on a casual or temporary basis. Author's collection.

APPENDIX IV

Conditions of Employment and Welfare 1869 to 1913

The employees of the MB&M were covered by various schemes to promote their welfare. From the start of the railway, there appears to have been a voluntary scheme whereby employees became members of a Mutal Provident Society and in 1876 the MC made an ex-gratia funeral allowance to a goods porter at Bollington who had not been on the permanent staff long enough to entitle him to a funeral allowance from the Society. This in all probability was the Manchester, Sheffield and Lincolnshire Railway Provident Fund and Accident Fund, and was what was later to become the Great Central Railway and Joint Lines Friendly Society, which was established on 1 July 1866 and which provided a range of sickness, accident, and funeral benefits. The introduction of the Workmen's Compensation Act 1898 removed the obligations to provide for financial help following accidents at work. From 2 June 1899 the GC decided to subscribe 7½% of members' contributions. The 1911 scales show, for example, members' contributions of 10d. per week (for those joining over 30 and under 35 years of age and with weekly earnings of more than 15s.), a sick benefit for the first 6 months of 10s. a week, a pension of 3s. per week, and a funeral allowance of £12. The Medical Officers at that time were, for Rose Hill, High Lane and Middlewood, Dr. H. Burton, of Redlands, Marple; for Poynton and Bollington, Dr. D. W. Main of Bollington, and for Macclesfield, Dr. J. N. Laird of Fairstead House, Macclesfield. The employees on the MB&M formed part of the Woodley District for the election of a representative to the Committee of Management, and this District also included employees of "Stations on the Peak Forest and Macclesfield Canals".

In February 1881 the MC became parties to the Railway Clearing House Superannuation Fund. In February 1905 the MC decided that the employees should not be in the proposed GC Superannuation Fund though they did come in later.

Buttons and cap badges are from the E. Higgs collection, photograph by D. J. Frogatt.

Metal badge clipped to the front of cap. Author's collection.

Very little is known about the determining of wages and conditions in the early years of the MB&M. Employees were members of the various trade unions right from the start. In April 1913, wages of all employees came under the North Staffordshire Railway Conciliation Board C and the table below shows rates of pay for all grades of staff.

CONDITIONS OF SERVICE, COACHING DEPARTMENT

Weekly wages

Station	*Foremen* (Platform and Parcels) Minimum	*Foremen* (Platform and Parcels) Maximum	*Porters* (Platform and Parcels) Minimum	*Porters* (Platform and Parcels) Maximum	*Daily hours*
Bollington			8s.	18s. 6d.	12
High Lane			8s.	18s. 6d.	12
Macclesfield (Central)	23s.	30s.	8s.	19s. 6d.	10
Middlewood			8s.	18s. 6d.	12
Poynton			8s.	18s. 6d.	12
Rose Hill			8s.	18s. 6d.	12

CONDITIONS OF SERVICE OF SIGNALMEN

Cabin	*Class*	*Station*	*Weekly wages* Minimum	*Weekly wages* Maximum	*Annual Bonus*	*Daily hours*
Station	3rd	Bollington	23s.	24s	—	10
Mortar Mill	Extra 2nd	Macclesfield (Central)	29s.	30s.	£2 12s.	8
Goods Yard	2nd	Macclesfield (Central)	27s.	28s.	—	10
Goods Siding	2nd	Macclesfield (Central)	27s.	28s.	—	10
High Level Junction	3rd	Middlewood	23s.	24s.	—	10
Station	3rd	Poynton	23s.	24s.	—	10
Station	3rd	Rose Hill	23s.	24s.	—	10

April 1913 rates of pay. Author's collection.

NORTH STAFFORDSHIRE RAILWAY. 194
(CONCILIATION BOARD "C.")

CONDITIONS OF SERVICE

Of Weekly Staff permanently employed in the Coaching Department at **Macclesfield (Central)** Station.

Great Central and North Staffordshire Railway Committee.

Grade	Wages per Week Minimum	Wages per Week Maximum
Foreman	23/-	30/-
Porters...	8/-	19/6

Wages.

As per list, advancing 1/- per week per annum until maximum is reached (except Junior Porters, see below), subject to efficiency and conduct having been satisfactory.

Junior Porters.

Will be paid on the following scale :—

Age	14	15	16	17	18	19
Wages	8/-	9/-	11/-	13/-	15/	17/6

The maximum pay for adult Platform Porters twenty years of age to be 19/6.

Standard Hours of Duty.

Ten hours per day, exclusive of one hour for meals.

Overtime.

Each day to stand by itself, and rate-and-a-quarter to be paid for all time worked over the daily standard hours.

Sunday Duty.

Men called on duty between the hours of midnight Saturday and midnight Sunday, to be paid at the rate of time-and-a-quarter, with a minimum of half a day's pay for one call at the Sunday rate, and for two or more calls not less than a day's pay at the Sunday rate. This does not apply to men completing their week's work. Overtime to be paid after completing the standard hours of duty.

Good Friday and Christmas Day.

Men to work as required. Ordinary rate of pay whether working or not.

Temporary Duty.

A man temporarily employed in a higher grade for a day or more, to be paid at the minimum rate for that grade, in any case the allowance to be not less than at the rate of 1/- per week.

Holidays.

Foremen will be allowed six days' holiday, and porters four days' annually, with pay, providing conduct has been satisfactory during the previous twelve months.

Lodgings.

An allowance of 1/- per day or 1/6 for day and night will be made when on duty away from home.

Uniform.

Will be supplied in accordance with the Company's regulations.

BY ORDER.

A porter at Bollington yard with a GC wagon in the rear. The emblem on the cap is MB&M. A. Wrigley collection.

APPENDIX V

Railway Tickets of the MB&M

Railway tickets for travel originating on the MB&M were issued by the Macclesfield Committee, the Great Central and North Staffordshire Railway Committee, the LNE, and by British Railways. Note the different spellings and abbreviations used. As late as 1964, tickets printed in the form of "GC & Ns Jt com" were still being issued, 34 years after that Committee ceased to exist. The tickets below are a representative sample of dozens of different types that were issued, some of which are now in the hands of private collectors.

Tickets are from the collections of D. Geldard, M. G. Stewart and G. P. Waite.

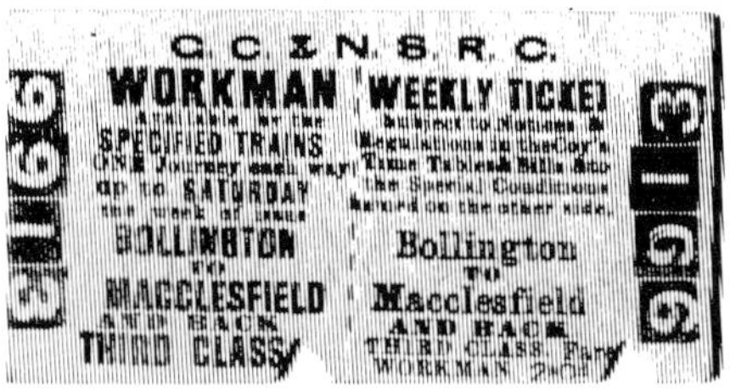

Hand lamp to MS&L design, over-stamped "MB&M RY", as used by permanent way staff. A. Turner collection.

Former LMS 2–6–4T, 42397, of Macclesfield shed, on a permanent way train between Rose Hill and High Lane on 31 August 1958. Bull head rail is being replaced by flat bottom spiked rail. R. Keeley.

APPENDIX VI
Operating and Maintenance

The complicated nature of running a railway owned by two different companies with their own regulations is best illustrated through the procedures for operating and maintenance. Right from the beginning the rules and regulations for operating the MB&M were those of the MS&L, and the Board successively adopted the changes in rules and regulations of the MS&L, GC, and LNE. Specific operating details on the MB&M were contained in the Appendices to the Working Timetables of the respective parent companies and were obviously the subject of discussion between them.

The maintenance of the line was under the control of the NS, and later the LMS, from Stoke. The permanent way maintenance was organised from the early days through 6 gangs – No. 1 from Macclesfield Central to Hurdsfield including exchange sidings and the goods yard; No. 2 to the start of the viaduct at Bollington; No. 3 to Adlington; No. 4 to just beyond Higher Poynton station; No. 5 to Torkington Road; and No. 6 to Rose Hill. This arrangement lasted until BR days, although gang sizes were reduced; by 1965 there were 3 gangs of 3 men each at Rose Hill, Higher Poynton and Bollington, and a gang of 6 at Macclesfield. The MB&M, from the beginning, paid the Sheffield and Midland Railway Companies Committee (and later the Great Central and Midland) a proportion of the costs of operating and maintaining the signal box and complex at Marple Wharf Junction; similarly the MB&M paid the NS a proportion for operating and maintaining the junctions in Macclesfield at Mortar Mill (Central South) signal box and at Macclesfield Junction signal box. The GC turntable at Macclesfield was oiled once a week by Stoke men, and certainly in the 1930's track for relaying came from Dewsnap, but was relaid by men from Stoke.

The responsibility of maintaining the Middlewood curve was the subject of dispute between the L&NW and the NS. It went to arbitration and a report was received from one James Grierson on 31 May 1886 in the following terms – the NS were to maintain and keep in repair at their own cost the signals at the north and south ends and the junctions, and, as to maintenance of any connections with the NS, apart from the junctions, and forms part of the station works, these were to be maintained at the cost of the MC. Until BR times, the curve was maintained by employees of the MB&M and the costs re-charged to the L&NW and NS, and later the LMS. The responsibility for engineering and design on the MB&M remained at Stoke until the closure of Stoke drawing office in the early 1950's, when it was transferred to Manchester.

Arrangements for breakdowns will have varied down the years. For example, on the Middlewood curve, the 1920 regulations show that trains broken down would be the responsibility of the L&NW breakdown gang at Longsight. The 1947 regulations show that both LMS and LNE trains on the MB&M from the junction at Macclesfield to Marple Wharf Junction were the responsibility of the LNE breakdown gang, including 45 ton steam crane, from Gorton.

Bridge plate from Torkington Road bridge. *I. R. Smith.*

Staff at High Lane, c. 1905. Front left is Tom Hallworth, platelayer; Sam Smith on the front row with a dog on his knees was foreman platelayer and next to him is Bill Smith, another platelayer. On the right of the back row is Jim Pickstone, another platelayer, and next to him Joe Bennett, a porter. The late F. Hallworth collection.

This family shot at Middlewood on 30 March 1959 shows the gradient post on the left and the boundary marker showing to the right the limit to maintenance responsibility on the MB&M. Behind can be seen the Middlewood brickworks.
J. W. Sutherland.

Trespass notice to an NS design, as is the station nameboard in the background.
N. F. W. Dyckhoff.

APPENDIX VII

Working the Line

Signal Box Closing Hours

Extract from Appendix No. 3, 1 November 1897, to Great Central Railway Working Timetable

Rose Hill	Closed Sunday between trains to 6.30 a.m. Monday.
High Lane	Closed after the passing of the last passenger train to 9 a.m. on weekdays; and on Saturday after the passing of the 6.55 p.m. train, Manchester to Macclesfield, to 9 a.m. Monday.
Middlewood Junction	Closed after last stopping Passenger Train to 7 a.m. weekdays; and on Saturday after the passing of the last stopping Passenger train to 7 a.m. Monday.
Poynton	Closed after the last Passenger train to 6.30 a.m.
Bollington	Closed Sunday between trains to 6.30 a.m. Monday.
Macclesfield Goods Junction	Closed after the passing of the last booked goods train on Sunday to 5.30 a.m. Monday.
Macclesfield Sidings	Closed between trains on Sunday to 5.30 a.m. Monday.

Rose Hill, Bollington, Macclesfield Goods Junction and Macclesfield Sidings signal boxes must be opened on Sundays 20 minutes before each train is booked to pass.

Catch Points

Extract from January 1908 Appendix to Great Central Railway Working Timetable

		Gradient
Marple Wharf Junction	On the Up Line, 94 yards South of the Signal Box, opposite the Down Home Signal.	1 in 220
High Lane	On the Up Line, 658 yards North of the Station.	1 in 116
Middlewood	On the Up Line, 118 yards South of the Up Home Signal.	1 in 218
Macclesfield Goods Junction	On the Down Line, 349 yards North of the Junction	1 in 77

Water Columns

Extract from January 1914 Appendix to Great Central Railway Working Timetable

Macclesfield	South end of Station Platform.	Up Line
	North end of Station Platform.	Down Line
	Goods Yard.	Sidings
Poynton	North end of Station Platform..	Down Line
	South end of Station Platform.	Up Line

Turntable

Macclesfield Length of Rail 44′ 10″

Speed Restrictions

Per Manchester, Sheffield and Lincolnshire Railway, 1889.

Extract from 1889 Appendix to Macclesfield, Sheffield and Lincolnshire Railway Working Timetable

Marple Wharf Junction	10 miles per hour

Extract from 1908 Appendix to Great Central Railway Working Timetable

Round the curve into Macclesfield Yard	15 miles per hour

Extract from 1937 Western Division Sectional Appendix to London, Midland and Scottish Railway Working Timetable

Between Marple and Macclesfield, except as shown	45 miles per hour
Through Marple Junction	15 miles per hour
Between Marple Junction and 10¾ miles past Rose Hill	20 miles per hour
Through Middlewood Curve and Junction to and from Buxton line	20 miles per hour
Between Macclesfield (Central) and ½ mile past, and round curve	15 miles per hour

Distance Signal Box to Signal Box

Miles	Yards	Name of Box
		Marple, Wharf Junction.
	1714	Rose Hill Station.
1	1689	High Lane Station.
	935	Middlewood Junction (334 yards to L&NW signal box).
	1248	Poynton Station.
4	336	Bollington Station.
1	1412	Macclesfield Goods Junction.
Until 1928	339	Macclesfield Sidings.
Until 1934	475	Macclesfield Junction.
	271	Macclesfield Central (South) also known as Macclesfield Mortar Mill.
From 1934	952	Macclesfield (Central) Station.

From 1928, at Macclesfield Exchange Sidings, there was a ground frame, electrically controlled from the Goods Junction signal box. The original signal box at the south end of the up platform at Macclesfield (Central) was replaced sometime between 1898 and 1907 by another signal box 50 yards or so to the south.

APPENDIX VIII
Station Facilities

This list is representative of arrangements for station advertising, station bookstalls, vending machines and the like.

26 June 1873:	Refreshment rooms at Macclesfield let to a Mr. Delamere, at a rental of 10% of gross takings.
17 April 1883:	Refreshment rooms let to Spiers and Pond on the same basis.
10 December 1886:	Automatic weighing machine rented at £10 p.a.
7 June 1889:	Agreement with W. H. Smith for privileges of advertising on outside space.
9 October 1896:	Agreement with W. H. Smith for advertising and bookstall privileges; the rental to be 5% on bookstall sales and 50% on advertisements.
13 February 1901:	Sweetmeat Automatic Delivery Company allowed to place 7 sweetmeat and machines at a rental of £30 p.a.
24 June 1920:	Wymans take over from W. H. Smith for 10 years from 1 January 1921.
25 October 1923:	Name stamping machine installed by Sweetmeat under a one-year agreement.
14 October 1930:	Bookstall agreement for 21 years with W. H. Smith.
9 December 1930:	LNE takes over exclusive rights of commercial advertising.

Signal box diagram of the signalling arrangements at Rose Hill, 1916. Note the later inking in, on the right, of the arrangements for the Park and Paterson sidings, installed in 1919. British Rail.

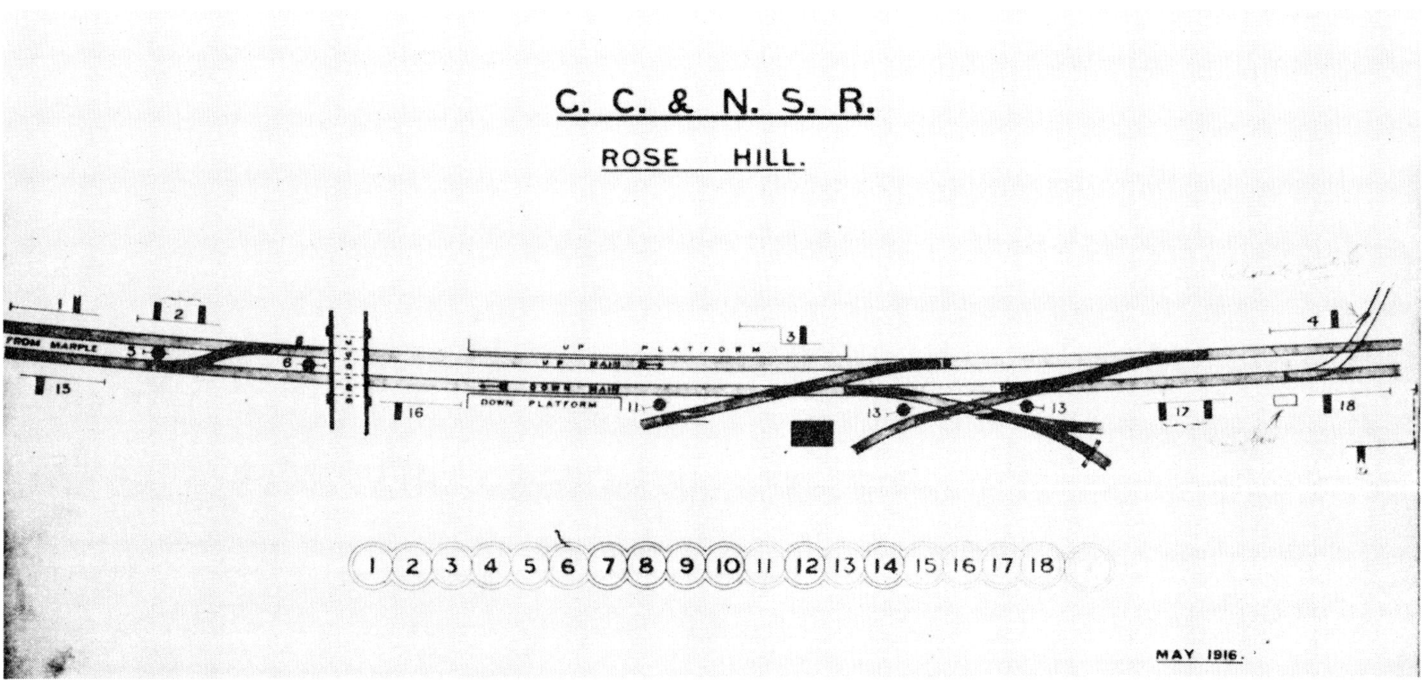

APPENDIX IX
Petrol Electric Railcar Daily Roster 1928

FROM BOLLINGTON	FROM MACCLESFIELD (CENTRAL)
7.23 a.m.	8.38 a.m.
9.15 a.m.	9.45 a.m.
10.45 a.m.	11.05 a.m.
11.25 a.m.	11.50 a.m. (to Higher Poynton - SO)
12.25 p.m. (12.18 p.m. - SO - from Higher Poynton)	1.00 p.m.
1.29 p.m. - SX	2.00 p.m.
1.45 p.m. - SO	
2.30 p.m.	3.00 p.m.
3.20 p.m.	3.35 p.m. - SO
3.53 p.m. - SO	4.30 p.m.
4.50 p.m.	5.00 p.m. - SO
	5.15 p.m. - SX
5.30 p.m.	6.00 p.m. - SO
6.12 p.m. - SX	6.50 p.m.
7.00 p.m. - SX	8.00 p.m. to Romily - SX Woodley - SO
7.05 p.m. - SX	
8.36 p.m. - SX from Romiley	
8.41 p.m. - SO from Woodley	9.30 p.m.
9.50 p.m.	10.13 p.m.
	10.45 p.m. - SX
10.25 p.m.	10.57 p.m. (to Higher Poynton - SO)

SO - Saturdays only. SX - Saturdays excepted.

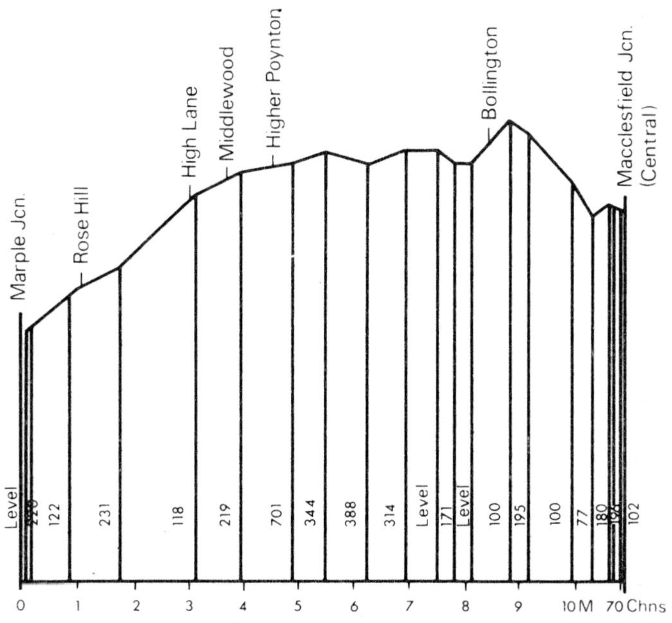

APPENDIX X

Passenger Timetable July to September 1887

UP	WEEKDAYS									SUNDAYS			
	a.m.	a.m.	a.m.	p.m.	p.m.	p.m.	p.m.	p.m.	p.m.	a.m.	a.m.	p.m.	p.m.
Manchester (London Road)	7.45	9.25	10.35	1.30	2.20	4.20	5.40	6.50	10.30	7.00	9.55	2.10	6.50
Marple (Rose Hill)	8.14	9.15	11.10	1.53	3.26	4.43	6.05	7.15	11.11	7.43	10.33	2.48	7.23
High Lane	8.19	9.56	11.15	1.58	3.31	4.48	6.10	7.20	11.16	7.48	10.38	2.53	7.28
Middlewood	8.22	—	11.18	2.01	3.34	(c)	(c)	7.23	—	—	—	—	—
Poynton	8.25	10.01	11.21	2.04	3.37	4.53	6.15	7.26	11.20	7.52	10.42	2.57	7.32
Bollington	8.33	10.09	11.29	2.12	3.45	5.01	6.23	7.34	11.28	8.00	10.50	3.05	7.40
Macclesfield (Central)	8.40	10.16	11.36	2.19	3.52	5.08	6.30	7.41	11.35	8.07	10.57	3.12	7.47
				Sat. only		*Sat. exc.*			*Sat. only*				
	(b)	*(b)*	*(a)*	*(b)*	*(a)*	*(b)*	*(b)*	*(b)*	*(a)*				

(a) via Guide Bridge route.
(b) via Reddish route.
(c) stops when required.

DOWN	WEEKDAYS									SUNDAYS		
	a.m.	a.m.	a.m.	p.m.	p.m.	p.m.	p.m.	p.m.	p.m.	a.m.	p.m.	p.m.
Macclesfield (Central)	7.10	9.00	10.50	1.40	4.10	5.57	7.10	9.30	8.30	12.45	4.15	8.40
Bollington	7.15	9.05	10.55	1.45	4.15	6.02	7.15	9.35	8.35	12.50	4.20	8.45
Poynton	7.23	9.13	11.03	1.53	4.23	6.10	7.23	9.43	8.43	12.58	4.28	8.53
Middlewood	7.26	9.16	(c)	1.56	4.26	6.13	7.26	—	—	—	—	—
High Lane	7.29	9.19	11.09	1.59	4.29	6.16	7.29	9.49	8.48	1.03	4.33	8.58
Marple (Rose Hill)	7.34	9.24	11.14	2.04	4.34	6.21	7.34	9.54	8.53	1.08	4.38	9.03
Manchester (London Road)	8.03	9.47	11.35	2.45	5.15	6.50	8.03	10.50	9.33	1.48	5.18	9.43
	(b)	*(b)*	*(b)*	*(a)*	*(a)*	*(b)*	*(b)*	*(a)*	*(a)*	*(a)*	*(a)*	*(a)*

(a) via Guide Bridge route.
(b) via Reddish route.
(c) stops when required.

Passenger Timetable - 3 October 1921

UP	WEEKDAYS													SUNDAYS			
	a.m.	a.m.	a.m.	a.m.	a.m.	p.m.	p.m.	p.m.	p.m.	p.m.	p.m.	p.m.	p.m.	a.m.	a.m.	p.m.	p.m.
Manchester (London Road)	6.50	7.20	8.43	9.05	11.00	12.21 *(from) Ashburys)*	12.40	12.50	1.40	4.25	5.45	7.05	10.20	6.50	10.00	2.00	6.35
Rose Hill (Marple)	7.22	8.05	9.28	9.35	11.44	12.44	1.09	1.41	2.25	4.55	6.12	7.35	10.50	7.32	10.42	2.52	7.16
High Lane	7.27	8.12	9.33	—	11.49	—	1.14	1.46	2.30	5.00	6.17	7.40	10.55	7.37	10.47	2.57	7.21
Middlewood	—	8.20	9.36	—	11.52	—	1.17	1.49	2.33	5.03	6.20	7.43	—	—	—	—	—
Poynton (for Lyme Park)	7.33	8.25	9.41	—	11.57	—	1.22	1.54	2.38	5.09	6.25	7.48	11.02	7.44	10.53	3.05	7.28
Bollington	7.40	8.32	9.48	—	12.04	—	1.29	2.02	2.45	5.18	6.32	7.55	11.09	7.51	11.00	3.13	7.35
Macclesfield (Central)	7.46	8.38	9.54	—	12.10	—	1.35	2.02	2.51	5.24	6.38	8.01	11.15	7.57	11.06	3.19	7.41
						Sat. only	*Sat. only*		*Sat. only*	*Sat. exc.*			*Wed & Sat only*				
	(b)	*(a)*	*(a)*	*(b)*	*(a)*	*(b)*	*(b)*	*(a)*	*(a)*	*(b)*	*(b)*	*(b)*	*(b)*	*(a)*	*(a)*	*(a)*	*(a)*

DOWN	WEEKDAYS										SUNDAYS			
	a.m.	a.m.	a.m.	a.m.	a.m.	p.m.	p.m.	p.m.	p.m.	p.m.	a.m.	p.m.	p.m.	p.m.
Macclesfield (Central)	6.13	7.20	9.00	—	10.35	12.30	2.20	3.50	6.00	7.30	8.15	12.30	4.00	9.00
Bollington	6.20	7.29	9.07	—	10.42	12.37	2.27	3.57	6.07	7.37	8.26	12.37	4.07	9.08
Poynton (for Lyme Park)	6.29	7.38	9.16	—	10.51	12.46	2.36	4.06	6.16	7.46	8.35	12.46	4.16	9.17
Middlewood	—	7.41	9.19	—	10.54	12.49	2.39	4.09	6.19	7.49	—	—	—	—
High Lane	6.33	7.44	9.22	—	10.57	12.52	2.42	4.12	6.22	7.52	8.40	12.51	4.21	9.22
Rose Hill (Marple)	6.38	7.49	9.28	9.05	11.02	12.57	2.47	4.17	6.29	7.57	8.47	12.56	4.26	9.28
Manchester (London Road)	7.08	8.33	9.52	10.30	11.31	1.26	3.18	4.46	6.57	8.30	9.36	1.37	5.06	10.15
							Sat. only							
	(b)	*(a)*	*(b)*	*(a)*	*(b)*	*(b)*	*(b)*	*(b)*	*(b)*	*(b)*	*(a)*	*(a)*	*(a)*	*(a)*

(a) via Guide Bridge route.
(b) via Reddish route.

Passenger Timetable - 1 September 1944

UP	WEEKDAYS																	SUNDAYS				
	a.m.	a.m.	a.m.	a.m.	a.m.	p.m.	p.m.	p.m.	p.m.	p.m.	p.m.	p.m.	p.m.	p.m.	p.m.	p.m.	p.m.	a.m.	a.m.	p.m.	p.m.	p.m.
Manchester (London Road)	6.22	6.58	7.40	8.43	10.35	12.10	12.42	12.55	12.52	1.50	3.10	4.25	5.11	5.45	6.27	7.15	10.45	7.03	9.50	1.20	5.10	7.05
Rose Hill (Marple)	7.09	8.45	8.11	9.26	11.18	12.41	1.12	1.38	1.41	2.33	3.48	4.55	5.40	6.18	6.56	7.47	11.13	7.42	10.18	1.56	5.51	7.42
High Lane	7.14	—	8.16	9.31	11.23	12.46	1.17	1.43	1.46	2.38	3.53	5.00	5.45	6.23	—	7.52	11.18	7.48	10.23	2.01	5.56	7.47
Middlewood	7.17	—	8.21	9.34	11.26	12.49	1.20	1.46	1.49	2.41	3.56	5.03	5.48	6.26	—	7.55	—	—	10.26	2.04	5.59	7.50
Higher Poynton	7.22	—	8.26	9.39	11.31	12.54	1.25	1.51	1.54	2.46	4.01	5.09	5.52	6.30	—	8.00	11.26	7.56	10.30	2.09	6.04	7.55
Bollington	7.30	—	8.34	9.46	11.38	1.01	1.32	1.58	2.02	2.53	4.08	5.18	5.59	6.37	—	8.07	11.33	8.03	10.37	2.16	6.11	8.02
Macclesfield (Central)	7.38	—	8.40	9.52	11.47	1.07	1.41	2.04	2.08	2.59	4.14	5.24	6.09	6.43	—	8.14	11.39	8.09	10.37	2.22	6.17	8.08
						Sat. only	*Sat. only*	*Sat. exc.*	*Sat. only*	*Sat. only*		*Sat. exc.*	*Sat. exc.*		*Sat. exc.*		*Sat. only*					
	(a)	*(b)*	*(a)*	*(a)*	*(a)*	*(b)*	*(b)*	*(a)*	*(a)*	*(a)*	*(a)*	*(b)*	*(b)*	*(b)*	*(b)*	*(b)*	*(b)*	*(a)*	*(b)*	*(a)*	*(a)*	*(a)*

(a) via Guide Bridge route.
(b) via Reddish route.

DOWN	WEEKDAYS																SUNDAYS				
	a.m.	a.m.	a.m.	a.m.	a.m.	p.m.	p.m.	p.m.	p.m.	p.m.	p.m.	p.m.	p.m.	p.m.	p.m.	p.m.	a.m.	a.m.	p.m.	p.m.	p.m.
Maccesfield (Central)	6.11	7.18	—	8.08	10.38	12.25	1.20	2.25	3.48	4.30	5.43	6.23	6.37	—	9.00	10.15	8.23	11.00	3.56	6.57	8.23
Bollington	6.18	7.26	—	8.15	10.45	12.32	1.27	2.32	3.55	4.37	5.50	6.30	6.44	—	9.07	10.22	8.30	11.07	4.03	7.04	8.30
Higher Poynton	6.27	7.33	—	8.22	10.54	12.41	1.36	2.41	4.04	4.46	5.59	6.39	6.53	—	9.16	10.31	8.38	11.15	4.12	7.12	8.39
Middlewood	6.30	7.36	—	8.25	10.57	12.44	1.39	2.44	4.07	4.49	6.02	6.42	6.56	—	9.19	—	—	11.18	4.15	7.15	8.42
High Lane	6.33	7.39	—	8.28	11.00	12.47	1.42	2.47	4.10	4.52	6.05	6.45	6.59	—	9.22	10.35	8.44	11.21	4.18	7.18	8.45
Rose Hill (Marple)	6.38	7.44	8.21	8.32	11.05	12.52	1.47	2.52	4.15	4.57	6.10	6.50	7.04	7.16	9.27	10.40	8.49	11.26	4.23	7.23	8.50
Manchester (London Road)	7.06	8.15	8.52	8.59	11.34	1.19	2.18	3.17	4.44	5.25	6.34	7.18	7.29	7.59	9.52	11.08	9.27	11.53	5.01	8.02	9.27
							Sat. only	*Sat. only*			*Sat. exc.*		*Sat. exc.*	*Sat. exc.*							
	(b)	*(a)*	*(b)*	*(b)*	*(b)*	*(b)*	*(b)*	*(b)*	*(b)*	*(b)*	*(b)*	*(b)*	-	*(a)*	*(b)*	*(b)*	*(a)*	*(b)*	*(a)*	*(a)*	*(a)*

(a) via Guide Bridge route.
(b) via Reddish route.

Minutes, cash books, ledgers, journals of the Macclesfield, Bollington and Marple Railway, the Macclesfield Committee, the Great Central and North Staffordshire Railway Committee, the London and North Eastern Railway and London, Midland and Scottish Railway Group Committee No. 1. *P.R.O.*

Deposited plans and Acts of Parliament relating to the Macclesfield, Bollington and Marple Railway *C.R.O.*

Minutes of the Bollington Local Board of Health and of the Bollington Urban District Council. *C.R.O.*

Minutes of the Marple Local Board of Health and of the Marple Urban District Council. *Stockport Borough Archive Office.*

Line drawings and Plans, Macclesfield, Bollington and Marple Railway and the Middlewood curve. *British Rail Property Board, Manchester.*

Minutes of the Joint London and North Western Railway and North Staffordshire Railway Committee. *P.R.O.*

Board of Trade Railway Inspectors' Reports. *P.R.O.*

Engineering Plans. *British Rail Civil Engineers, Manchester.*

Annual Reports, Poynton Collieries. *C.R.O.*

Cheshire Lines Committee Working Timetables. *N.R.M.*

Cheshire Lines Committee Working Timetables, Passenger Timetables, and Special Traffic Notices. *P.R.O.*

London and North Western Railway Working Timetables and Sectional Appendices, and Great Central Railway Working Timetables and Appendices. *P.R.O. and N.R.M.*

Manchester, Sheffield and Lincolnshire Railway, Sectional Appendix. *P.R.O.*

London, Midland and Scottish Railway, London and North Eastern Railway, Passenger Timetables, Working Timetables and Sectional Appendices, and British Rail Working and Passenger Timetables. *P.R.O.*

North Staffordshire Railway Working Timetables. *P.R.O.*

Miscellaneous records and papers, Middlewood station. *Stockport Borough Archive Office.*

Manchester, Sheffield and Lincolnshire Railway rosters and diagram workings. *Manchester Central Reference Library.*

Station Closure Proposals. *Transport Users' Consultative Committee, Manchester.*

P.R.O. *Public Record Office, Kew.*
C.R.O. *Cheshire Record Office, Chester.*
N.R.M. *National Railway Museum, York.*